Walking Wester Ross

Clan Walk Guides

Walking
Wester Ross

Walking Scotland Series
Volume 3

Mary Welsh
and
Christine Isherwood

First published by Westmorland Gazette 1991,
under the title *Walks in Wester Ross*

Revised edition published by Clan Books 1999

Second edition published by Clan Books 2003

Revised edition, 2006

Reprinted with revisions 2011

ISBN 978 1 873597 28 6

**Text and Illustrations
© Mary Welsh
and Christine Isherwood 2003**

**Clan Books
Clandon House
The Cross, Doune
Perthshire
FK16 6BE**

Printed and bound in Great Britain by
Bell & Bain Ltd., Glasgow

Publisher's Note

This collection of walks has maintained its position as one of the most popular volumes in the *Walking Scotland Series* since its first appearance in 2003. The opportunity of a reprint has been taken to check the walks and to amend the text of several chapters to reflect recent changes.

If, in spite of the authors' efforts, readers find anything incorrect or misleading in the text we shall be glad to be informed for future reference. However, it must be stated that the book sets out to be an entertaining and helpful guide, and neither the authors nor the the publishers can be held responsible for any loss or injury that might be considered to result from its use.

The Authors' Golden Rules for Good, Safe Walking

- Wear suitable clothes and take adequate waterproofs.

- Walk in strong footwear; walking boots are advisable.

- Carry the relevant map and a compass and know how to use them.

- Carry a whistle; remember six long blasts repeated at one minute intervals is the distress signal.

- Do not walk alone, and tell someone where you are going.

- If mist descends, return.

- Keep all dogs under strict control. Observe all "No Dogs" notices – they are there for very good reasons.

Contents

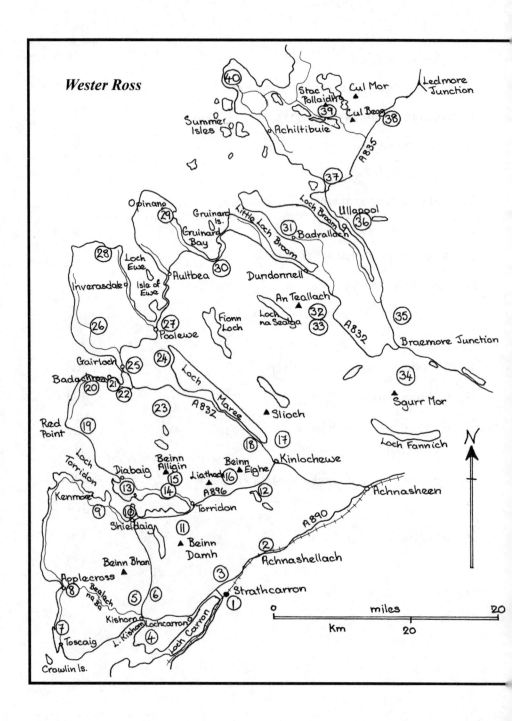

Achintee to Loch an Fheoir

Park in the station yard of Strathcarron, GR 942421. This is not a public car park nor does it belong to the railway. Make sure you do not block the access.

Beyond the head of **Loch Carron** lies broad, flat Strathcarron, surrounded by many low hills. On a sunny day, in the folds of the slopes, you come, unexpectedly, upon lochans sparkling, jewel-like, among the lonely hills. Hidden gorges carry tumbling burns, with many pleasing waterfalls and cascades as the rivers hurry towards Loch Carron.

Allt an-t Sagairt, Achintee

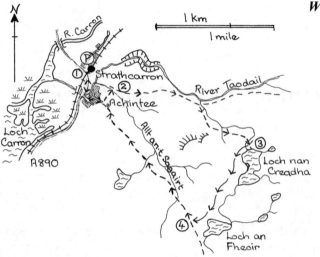

1. From the parking area, walk south-westwards for 300m along the A890. As you go look across the River Taodail to a row of holes high up on a sandstone cliff above the hurrying water. Watch the parent sand martins fly in and out, trying to satisfy their clamorous young. Then take the signposted left turn to climb the steep access road into the centre of the village of Achintee. Here follow a small footpath sign pointing down a side road to the left. After 100m turn right at another waymark to go up a reinforced track past the entrance to Park Cottage and on to pass an electricity substation. Go through a metal gate and carry on up the good track until you reach a drainage ditch. Do not cross but take the tiny footpath along the near bank to descend to stones to cross easily. Continue to the substantial stile over the deer fence ahead. Go on down the bank to the burn, the Allt an-t Sagairt, and cross on boulders. Climb the far bank and join a clear stalkers' path, where you turn right.

2. Continue uphill with, at first, the burn to your right but then leave it as you ascend a spur to come to some gateposts. Here bear left, with care, down a tiny path by the edge of the Taodail gorge, a wooded ravine 45m in depth, to a fine vantage point to see the two tiered waterfall, Eas an Teampuill, the temple fall. Legend has it that a temple existed here in early Christian times. Return to the main path and go on to a junction of paths, where you take the right branch. Climb steeply up beside, on your left, a tributary of the Taodail and then continue on the lower slopes of Creag Dhubh Bheag. Remain on the same side of the stream to come to the loch edge.

3. The next stretch of this walk is over pathless moorland, that can, at times, be very wet. If this is not for you return the same way. To continue, bear right alongside the pretty reeded loch, keeping well up the slopes. Stride on, without losing height, parallel with a feeder stream flowing from Loch an Fheoir, the loch that lies ahead. Continue beside this second loch, crossing a small tributary, to a clear track ahead.

4. Turn right and begin your long descent. Look for hoof prints of deer as you go. Enjoy the good views of Strathcarron, backed by wild mountain slopes as you descend. The way brings you to the new water treatment plant above Achintee. At the end of the enclosure, go down the bank onto the access track used at the outset of the walk and follow this downhill to the gate by the substation. Then retrace your steps back to the parking area.

Sand Martins

Practicals

Type of walk: A challenging, exhilarating walk up into the wild uplands above Achintee.

Distance: 4½ miles/7km

Time: 3 hours

Map: OS Explorer 429/OS Landranger 25

NB Do not attempt in the mist

2

Achnashellach, Coulin Pass, River Lair

Park in a large layby oppposite the phone box, GR 004584, at the entrance to the lane to Achnashellach station, which turns north off the A890. If approaching from the west, notice the shape of Fuar Tholl's ridge, which really does look live up to its nickname of Wellington's nose.

The **pine marten** was hunted in the Middle Ages. Groups of men on foot, with sticks and stones, took part in the national pastime of 'hunting the mart'. The marten has special scent glands near the base of the tail and secretes a musky odour. Unlike the polecat this odour does not disgust its enemy. One of its old English names was sweet marten to distinguish it from the foulmart or polecat. It feeds on rats,

Waterfall on the Easan Dorcha

mice voles, rabbits, young hares and game birds – it likes eggs too. It also eats caterpillars, beetles and carrion and has a taste for berries. As you walk look for a scattering of rowan berry skins, where the marten has sucked out the insides. You will also see some of these skins in his black twisted droppings on stones along the path. It was hunted almost to extinction at the beginning of the last century but is now making a good recovery.

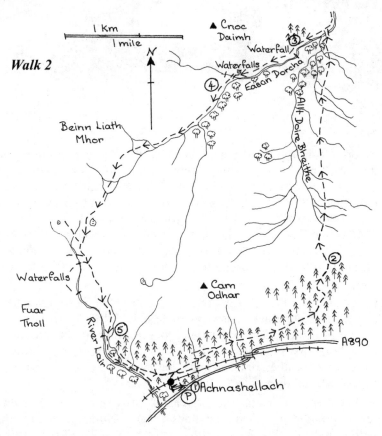

1. Walk up the tree-lined lane to the railway station. Cross the gated line, with care, and walk into Achnashellach Forest. At a signposted junction of several tracks, avoid the left and right turn and go ahead in the direction of the Coulin Pass. Stride the steadily climbing forest road through a variety of conifers from where come the whisperings of goldcrests and coal tits. Continue climbing the gently graded way, where you should watch out for red deer and the elusive pine marten.

11

Pine Marten

2. Emerge from the trees onto the Coulin Pass. Step out, north, along the rough road, with heather moorland on either side and enjoying the magnificent views ahead of the quartzite top of Beinn Eighe and the mass of Slioch. As you begin to descend Loch Coulin comes into view. Go on down and, just before you reach the bridge over the Easan Dorcha, look left to see a large area of fine Scots pine covering the far slopes. Cross the bridge and walk, left, upstream. Peer into the gorge, on the left, to see a plummeting waterfall descending white-topped under birch and pine.

3. Carry on along the clear path beside the tumbling burn. On the steep slopes, opposite, the extensive area of pines continues. Cross the next bridge over the Easan Dorcha and look right to see the magnificent waterfalls, overshadowed by birch and a huge Scots pine. About its banks grow heather, bracken and bilberry. Contine on the narrow path as it winds uphill beside the fall.

4. Follow the way as it starts to cross an extensive basin of moorland, littered with boulders. Soon the pines are left behind and the moorland path crosses the lower eastern skirts of Beinn Liath Mhor. Beyond, the view of mountains is magnificent. Gradually the path climbs out of the boulder field and goes on. Ignore both right turns and follow the cairned way. It begins to descend and from here you will soon spot Loch Dughaill far below. Carry on along the clear, boulder strewn path as it drops, unrelentingly, with the dramatic cliff-girt Fuar Tholl to the right. Just before the forest is reached, two short paths turn off right towards the bank of the River Lair. The first leads to a precarious viewpoint for the dramatic waterfalls racing down a drop in the tree-lined gorge. The second comes to a deep pool below spectacular cascades.

5 Walk past a notice board and then on into the forest, passing through a fence by a gateless gap. From now on the way is sheer magic. The easy path passes through glorious deciduous woodland, with the burn dancing and chattering beside you. Sheer mountain slopes crowd in on you with peak beyond peak to be seen to the right. Cross the sturdy footbridge over a hurrying tributary. Continue on to come to an arrowed board and a waymark, directing you left, to pass through a deer gate. Walk ahead on a good path repaired by the Footpath Trust to join a forest track. Turn right and descend steadily to pass through a kissing gate. Go on down the way to the cross of tracks passed early on the walk, swing right to descend to the railway line.

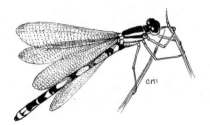

Common blue damselfly

Practicals

Type of walk: *An wonderful walk for good weather when the sun slants through the forest trees and the air, as you cross the moorland, is just moving enough to be invigorating.*

Distance: 9 miles/14.5km

Time: 5–6 hours

Maps: OS Explorer 429/OS Landranger 25

NB. Deer stalking takes place on the Achnashellach estate from Sept 15 to October 20 and the estate asks for minimal disturbance during that period. Contact the estate office stalker on 01520766266.

3

A walk around Maol Chean-dearg

Park in the small car park west of Coulags bridge, GR 956451, on the north side of the A890, between Achnashellach and Lochcarron. There is also space for one or two cars at the start of the walk

Lochcarron is a single long street of whitewashed cottages looking out across Loch Carron. It lies 5 miles west from where this walk starts, a walk that takes you into lonely heights and past deep blue lochs where sandpipers and red and black-throated divers feed. Look for sundew, butterwort and sweet gale in the wetter areas. Look too for the three members of the heather family – cross-leaved heath, bell heather and the wide spreading ling. Milkwort, tormentil and lousewort flourish on either side of the valley path. At the right time of the year you may see brightly coloured day-flying moths – Northern Eggar and the beautiful Emperor moth. You may find their large caterpillars in the heather.

Bothy, Sgorr Ruadh behind

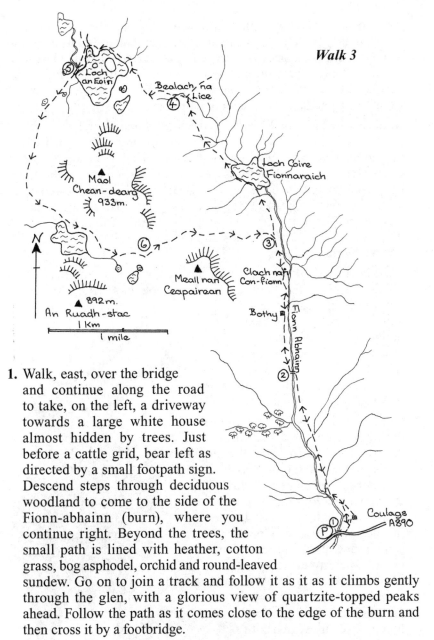

1. Walk, east, over the bridge
   and continue along the road
   to take, on the left, a driveway
   towards a large white house
   almost hidden by trees. Just
   before a cattle grid, bear left as
   directed by a small footpath sign.
   Descend steps through deciduous
   woodland to come to the side of the
   Fionn-abhainn (burn), where you
   continue right. Beyond the trees, the
   small path is lined with heather, cotton
   grass, bog asphodel, orchid and round-leaved
   sundew. Go on to join a track and follow it as it as it climbs gently
   through the glen, with a glorious view of quartzite-topped peaks
   ahead. Follow the path as it comes close to the edge of the burn and
   then cross it by a footbridge.

2. Turn right and head along the clear path, rough in places, deeper into
   the glen. It passes through a heather garden before reaching an old

croft house, shaded by a gnarled rowan, which has been restored by the Mountain Bothies Association to provide shelter for climbers and walkers. Follow the path as it carries on close to the left-hand bank of the burn. Then, where the path moves away from the hurrying water, look right to see the standing stone, Clach nan Con-fionn – a stone to which the legendary Fionn tethered his dogs.

3. At the cairned fork in the path, ignore the left branch and go on ahead through the glen, soon to come beside, on the right, Loch Coire Fionnaraich, where you will want to pause to enjoy this quiet corner. Then begin your climb towards the head of the glen and, at the cairn, bear left to ascend to the brow of the Bealach na Lice, shadowed occasionally by Maol Chean-dearg. Here in summer look for alpine lady's mantle and for bearberry and Arctic bearberry. Pause here to look down on several small lochans and the delightful Loch an Eoin, all cradled by rocky slopes.

4. Then begin your descent towards the loch, where in summer golden rod grows scattered between the large boulders, white lousewort thrives on the heather roots and here too procumbent juniper flourishes. Continue around the edge of the loch, with its pleasing small islands, to a cairn. Ignore the continuing path to Annat and turn left.

5. Climb steadily away from the loch. Watch out as you go for a sudden, unexpected view of Loch Carron and the mountains of Skye. Follow the path as it contours round the steep slopes of Maol Chean-dearg, where you might spot red deer high up on patchy grass. To the right in a hollow, lies Loch Coire an Ruadh-staic, reflecting the terraced barrenness of An Ruadh-stac beyond. The path continues climbing into a moon-like land-scape, passing a tiny lochan and then two more lovely lochans set in a quartzite bowl.

Stag roaring

16

6. As the path begins to curve left, east, and is still climbing, watch out for the easy-to-miss start of its long descent to the glen traversed at the outset of the walk. The way passes below the south slopes of Maol Chean-dearg, on the left, and the crags of Meall nan Ceapairean to the right. Follow the zig-zags that reduce the gradient and go on down to reach the cairn passed much earlier on the walk. To your right lies the standing stone and a glimpse of the chimney pots of the bothy. Turn right and begin your tramp back through the glen.

Emperor Moth

Black-thoated Diver

Practicals

Type of walk: *This is a really grand walk, with well defined paths and tracks for all the way. When the sun is shining the colour of the lochs and the dazzle of the quartzite is wonderful.*

Distance: 11½ miles/18.5km

Time: 6–7 hours

Maps: OS Explorer 429/OS Landranger 25

NB. Avoid this walk during the September to October stalking season.

4

Achintraid to Strome Castle

There are several places to park on the edge of the road, GR 840386 or 843393. Search for the best, taking care not to block passing places. To reach this leave the A896, Lochcarron to Shieldaig road, and turn left just past Kishorn, signposted Achintraid.

A gated footpath leads up to the courtyard of **Strome Castle**. Built in the 15th century, and demolished after a siege in 1602, it was originally part of the lands of the ancient earldom of Ross. In 1472 Celestine, son of Alexander, Earl of Ross, gave the castle to Alan Cameron of Lochiel. The charter was confirmed by James IV in 1495 but, in 1539, it was revoked by James V and the castle given to the Macdonalds of Glengarry.

From that time there was continual struggle for possession of the castle between the Macdonalds and their neighbours, the Mackenzies of Kintail. In 1602, Mackenzie laid siege to the castle. He was about to admit failure when women from the castle went out to draw water from the well. On their return, frightened and in a poor light, they poured the water into a vat containing gun-powder. When the defenders came to replenish their stock they discovered what had

Strome Castle

happened. A Mackenzie prisoner in the castle heard the Macdonalds cursing the women. He escaped and told his chief who immediately renewed the attack. The Macdonalds sued for peace, and were allowed to leave safely, whereupon the Mackenzies blew up the castle and it has remained a ruin ever since.

Walk 4

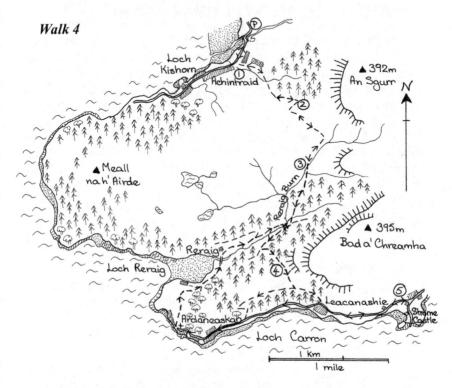

1. Opposite the post box in Achintraid take the track, signed Reraig and Leacanashie, and follow it uphill through broadleaved woodland, with a tiny burn below on the right. Ignore any side tracks and keep beside the burn, crossing it twice. Emerge from the trees by a gate onto the open moor. Go on along a much rougher track beside a forestry plantation and head on as it bears round to the left in the direction of the cliff-girt An Sgurr.

2. At an obvious cairn turn right at an acute angle and traverse the hillside, climbing gently, until you reach the top of the ridge marked by another large cairn. Pause here to look back and admire the fine view of the Applecross mountains, with the road to the Bealach na Ba snaking up the side of the leftmost valley. Then descend the

other side of the ridge on a long easy slant. There is a very boggy area in the bottom, where paths proliferate as everyone tries a new way round. Very soon the path becomes delightful as it follows the bank of the Reraig Burn, which tumbles in a series of pools and little falls. Cross the burn on stepping stones.

3. Continue down the path through scattered birch, with a deer fence and forest on your left to go through a rickety gate into the trees. Stroll the new well drained path, marked with pine marten droppings, as it continues through open birch woodland, with spruce and pine beyond. Pass through a small clear-felled area, cross a burn and go up the far side onto a forest track. Turn right and walk to a Y-junction. Branch left here, and after a bend about 200 metres along, take a path which goes left into the trees. (This may be waymarked, but the sign was missing when last checked.) The way climbs steeply through the forest and, near the top, emerges from the trees into an area of old clear-fell below a fine cliff. Look back again to enjoy the Applecross hills.

4. Press on from the ridge down the forest track to a cairn. Turn left and walk to a turning space at the end of the track. Look for the small waymark on a tree which directs you, right, along a path. Follow this down to the road. Turn left and walk through pleasant oak and birch wood, with lichened crags overhanging the road, for over a kilometre to a road junction. Turn right and go down to see the castle ruins and perhaps on to look at the slipway for the old Strome Ferry.

5. Return along the road, which is quiet and passes through more lovely woodland, to Leacanshie and then on to Ardaneaskan towards the end of the peninsula. In the small car park there is a conveniently placed seat with a splendid view of Skye and Plockton – just the place for a break. Return to the road and walk north to its end beyond the last cottage. Cross the cattle grid and follow the good reinforced track over the hill to Reraig. Continue above the shore, where you are likely to see herons, curlews and oystercatchers.

Heron

Cross the Reraig Burn on a concrete bridge and go on through two gates. Continue beside the burn into the forest, ignoring a branch to the left Cross the burn again on a good bridge to rejoin your outward track. Retrace your steps over the hill to Achintraid.

Spotted Flycatcher

Practicals

Type of walk: *A delightful walk of contrasts – woodland, moorland, seashore, riverside and a ruined castle.*

Distance:	8½ miles/13.5km
Time:	4–5 hours
Map:	OS Explorer 428/OS Landranger 24

5

Coire na Poite

Park on the wide firm verge, GR 835423, on the left of the road 1/2km beyond the junction before the bridge over the River Kishorn. To reach this, leave the A896 north of Kishorn, at Tornapress, to take the minor road to Applecross which goes over the Bealach na Ba.

Beinn Bhan is the highest mountain on the Applecross peninsula. At 896m it qualifies as a Corbett and is a massif of considerable stature. The whole mountain mass slopes upwards from south-west to north-east, ending suddenly in dramatic terraced sandstone cliffs gouged into great spectacular corries and hanging valleys by Ice Age glaciers. There are six corries on the north-east side of Beinn Bhan – from south to north they are Coire nan Each, Coire na Feola, Coire na Poite, Coire nan

a'Phoit, Beinn Bhan

22

Fhamhair, Coire Tell a'Bhein and Coire Gorm Beag. Coire na Poite, directly below the summit, is the most magnificent.

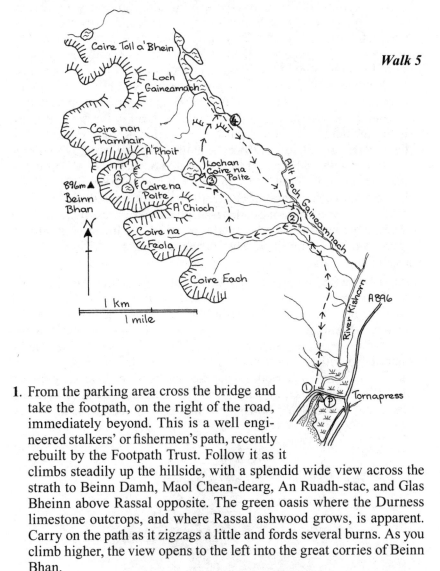

Walk 5

1. From the parking area cross the bridge and take the footpath, on the right of the road, immediately beyond. This is a well engineered stalkers' or fishermen's path, recently rebuilt by the Footpath Trust. Follow it as it climbs steadily up the hillside, with a splendid wide view across the strath to Beinn Damh, Maol Chean-dearg, An Ruadh-stac, and Glas Bheinn above Rassal opposite. The green oasis where the Durness limestone outcrops, and where Rassal ashwood grows, is apparent. Carry on the path as it zigzags a little and fords several burns. As you climb higher, the view opens to the left into the great corries of Beinn Bhan.

2. The path continues to a wooden bridge over a burn – but do not cross. Instead take the walkers' narrow path going uphill, with the burn on your right. This is boggy in places but quite clear. It appears

to be going into the second corrie, Coire na Feola, but above a waterfall turns right and fords the burn. Follow it over the high, boggy plateau towards a distinctive perched boulder topped with vegetation on the ridge ahead. The dramatic corries and cliffs are now on your left. Just before you reach the boulder your way is blocked by another burn – this one is the outflow from Lochan Coire na Poite. Turn left and follow it up into the outer corrie. This is one of those cases where you cross several low ridges as you climb up into the corrie, and you are sure each one is the last – only to find another beyond it. Eventually you do come over the final ridge and there is the lochan before you, mirroring the splendid rock scenery. The deep corrie on the left is Coire na Poite; it is enclosed by two precipitous ridges ending in great castellated buttresses – A'Chioch on the left and A' Phoit on the right. High in the corrie at the back is a lip concealing two small lochans, the haunt of several dippers. The burn from the lochans cascades down the rocks on the right. Behind them is the headwall of the corrie, which rises almost vertically to the summit of Beinn Bhan. The corrie to the right of A'Phoit is Coire nan Fhamhair.

3. After you have completed your survey of this dramatic hollow, cross the burn on stones just below the outflow from the lochan. Go on over the pebbly, sparsely vegetated hillside above the east side of the lochan, heading north. Go round the end of the low hill and descend to cross the beginning of another ridge, onto a wide shelf fringed at its outer edge with continuous slabs of Torridon sandstone. At the right hand end of this rock shelf is a shallow gully, which is an easy line of descent, though needing care through heather and boulders. (If you can't find this gully go down the gently sloping rock slabs until they

Dipper

Golden-ringed dragonfly

end above a burn, and follow the right bank of the burn down.) Both routes come down to the shore of Loch Gaineamhach, where you pick up a small path. Turn right and, very quickly, you reach the stalkers' path where it ends by the outflow from the loch

4. Follow the path all the way back down to the road at Tornapress. There is only one bridge, all other burns have to be forded.

Practicals

Type of walk: *An exhilarating challenge, with dramatic scenery for most of the way.*

Distance: 6 miles/9.5km
Time: 4 hours
Map: OS Explorer 428/OS Landranger 24

NB. A South-West Ross Deer Management Group sign at the start of the path asks you to avoid using the path during the stalking season (mid-August to mid-October) without previously contacting the stalker of the Applecross Estate, tel 01520 733249 or 01520 744247.

6

Rassal Ashwood

Park in a large layby off the road, GR 841432, on the east side of the A896, 3km north of Kishorn and 0.8km beyond the junction for the Bealach na Ba at Tornapress.

The **Rassal Ashwood National Nature Reserve** (85 hectares), established in 1956, lies to the north-west of Lochcarron and is the most northerly ashwood in Britain. Ash woodland has developed on this site because of the lime-rich soils formed on an outcrop of Durness limestone. The limestone forms ridges following the lines of bedding in the rock, with heavy clay soil lying in between. The main aim of the Nature conservancy council management on the reserve is to encourage the natural regeneration of the ashwood and its characteristic vegetation.

Rassal Ashwood

1. Go down the slope behind the layby, cross an iris bed and then a small burn. Walk up the grass to go through a kissing gate in a deer fence. Follow the narrow path uphill – in summer through beds of meadowsweet, with lady's mantle, self heal and devil's bit scabious. Follow the grassy path as it climbs through open woodland until you reach a junction. Turn left and continue through an open level area from where there is a fine view ahead of Beinn Damh. Carry on along the path as it winds round to the right, climbing again, and crosses two small burns.

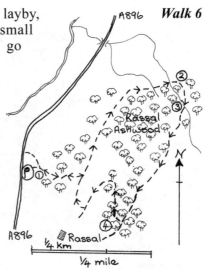

2. Continue on the path as it turns right again into the wood at a higher level, with ash trees growing out of a little limestone crag on the left. The open hillside above the wood has many small limestone outcrops and patches of bright green grass. This contrasts starkly, in autumn, with the purple-moor-grass-covered slopes on the opposite side of the valley, which are amber and deep brown. There are many splendid examples of elderly ash trees but not much between these and the very young saplings, which suggests that the area has not been fenced for long.

3. Recross the stream and go through a gap in an old limestone dyke. The path becomes a wide grassy ride, crossing several clearings where there is bracken. Above the ash trees to the right you can see Coire na Poite and the magnificent profile of Beinn Bhan. In the marshy areas look out for snipe and, in autumn, the trees are full of redwings and fieldfares. In spring water avens and violets flourish.

4. At a junction, take another wide grassy ride which is angled sharply back to the right. Follow it as it curves round and begins to descend quite steeply. Enjoy the view through the trees of soft, gentle woodland in the foreground, framing the stark corries and sandstone terraces of Beinn Bhan. Twenty metres before a gate in the deer fence, take a small path that goes off right. It brings you down to

27

Meadowsweet

the junction where you turned left earlier, thus completing the loop. Turn right and go down to the kissing gate with the sign, where you entered the wood. Go on to rejoin your car.

Practicals

Type of walk: *A delightful stroll through the rides of this unusual. wood.*

Distance:	1 mile/11.5km
Time:	1 hour
Map:	OS Explorer 428/OS Landranger 24

Ardban and Coillegillie

There is room at the start of the walk for 2–3 cars at the end of the track, GR 712400; otherwise the passing places before and after have extra spaces for 2–3 cars without blocking them. To reach this, drive 3 miles/5km south from Applecross, passing through Camusterrach to take the next right turn, signposted Ard Dhubh. The walk begins where a track leaves this road 1/4km further along.

Common seals abound on this walk, swimming or hauled out on the rocks, idly flapping at intruders who approach too near to their chosen resting places. You should also see a few Atlantic grey seals, identified by the Roman nose and large size. The common seal, with its dog-like face, is more timid than the very curious grey. If you are lucky you might also see an otter.

The Crowlin Islands lie off Toscaig across the Caolas Mor (Big Sound). They consist of three islands – Eilean Mor (Big Island), Eilean Mheadhonach (Middle Island) and Eilean Beag (Little Island). Between the big and middle is an extremely sheltered harbour and both islands are joined at low tide. People used to live on Eilean Mor – the ruins of houses are visible from the mainland.

Ardban

1. Take the good reinforced track which leaves the road, on the left, and is signposted Ardban and Coillegillie. Follow it as it crosses moorland, dips down to cross a burn and the climbs again through scattered birch. At the top of the hill pause to enjoy the view down over the headland of Ardban with its white cottages, and of Raasay with Skye behind. The sea is studded with skerries and islets; the largest of these is Eilean nan Naomh where St Maelrubha is said to have landed when he first arrived from Ireland.

Walk 7

2. Go on down the path beside a huge sloping slab of rock and continue where it descends steeply through birch and rowan woodland, with crags and boulders to the left and an inlet to the right. At the bottom of the slope take the right branch round the head of the inlet, signposted Ardban. The path, built like a stone jetty, goes along the west side of the inlet and then turns left over a rise and comes down to the green oasis of Ardban. In spring and summer look for golden plovers on the grassy meadow and ringed plovers on the shell sand beach. Look also for irises in the boggy areas and seals and otters in the sea about the rocks. Cross the grass to go round the headland, north to south, and return past the cottages to the shell sand beach.

3. Walk south along the turf behind the beach and at the end look for a roughly built stone well, just above the beach. Then follow a small path, possibly just an animal track, which contours round above the shore. It crosses a flat boggy area, winds round a knoll and dips to cross another boggy stretch about a tiny burn. Carry on the way as it climbs through a small birch wood and out round the hillside. There is a white sandy bay below and innumerable skerries. Continue on the path as it turns inland. Descend steeply through more birch woodland to join a substantial track, and turn right to go down to Coillegillie. The houses here are mainly ruins although two are still lived in. Go on beyond the houses to the headland and enjoy the view to the Crowlin Islands just across the bay with the Isle of Skye beyond.

4. Return up the well made path which is quite boggy at the start. Ignore the animal path you came along and slant down through the wood into a steep-sided valley. The good path goes down the left side, then crosses over lower down to bring you back to the signpost where you turned off to Ardban. Go up the hill through the wood and back over the moor to your car.

Common seal

Practicals

Type of walk: *A lovely easy walk in a glorious corner of Wester Ross. It takes you along mainly good tracks and paths. Some can be muddy after rain. There is a little cross country walking on faint paths or animal tracks.*

Distance: 3 miles/5km

Time: 2 hours or more if you wish to linger on the sandy beaches.

Map: OS Explorer 428/OS Landranger 24

8

Applecross

Park in the car park opposite the post office in Applecross, GR 712446. To reach this area use the coast road from Shieldaig or over the Bealach na Ba from Tornapress, north of Kishorn – both roads are narrow and tortuous but offer spectacular views – for the passengers.

There have been a large number of paths and routes on the Applecross peninsula for a number of years. A recent project has seen the revitalisation and extension of the network and resources have been provided by the Applecross Trust Estate, Ross and Cromarty Enterprise and Leader II. These resources were used to provide training in rural skills and as part of the project a number of paths have been constructed or repaired.

St Maelrubha came from Northern Ireland and, in 673 AD, founded a monastery in Applecross. The original Gaelic name for Applecross is A'Chomraich which means 'The Sanctuary'. Maelrubha went out from here to spread the word in much of the western Highlands and is second in regard only to St Columba. He died in 722 at the age of 80

Applecross

and is buried at Applecross, although it is not quite clear which stone marks his grave. The monastery was raided by Vikings in 795 and the church destroyed. The present church was built in 1817.

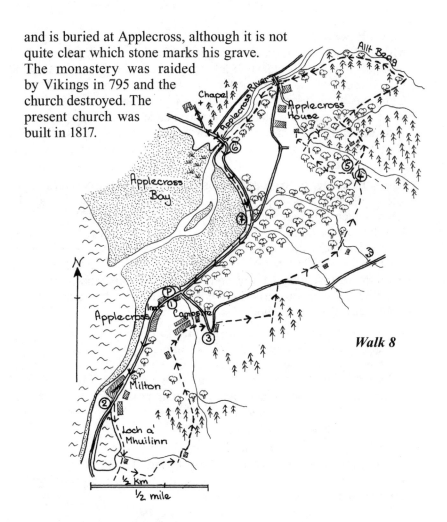

Walk 8

1. Return to the road from the car park and turn right. Go past the Applecross Inn and the row of white cottages fronting the sea, which makes up most of Applecross village. Beyond the cottages the road goes through a sycamore wood full of primroses and bluebells in the spring. The shore to the right consists of amazing slabs of Durness limestone. Ignore the road off to the right into the village of Milton and continue uphill. Pass a cottage on the left and take a track, on the left, just beyond it.

2. Go through a gate in the deer fence and on along the shore of Loch a' Mhuilinn (the Mill Loch). Pass through another deer gate and then

turn left beyond Lochend Cottage to take a path uphill, signposted Milton Walk. The gradient soon levels off and the path goes in front of a house named Torgarve to a kissing gate in a deer fence. Beyond follow the fence to the right for 5m then turn left on a good track. Continue through spruce to an iron kissing gate and then into open oak and birch woodland, with much coppiced hazel. Walk through the next gate and on in front of the farm steading at the Applecross campsite. Carry straight on to cross a burn and join the Bealach na Ba road at a hairpin bend.

3. Cross the corner of the road and keep to the left of the cottages opposite to follow a stepped path, signposted Smithy Woodland Walk. The forest which was here has been felled but the path is still clear. Turn left on the track at the top. Climb the stile over the deer fence and cross the road to take a diverging track on the far side. Beyond a cottage, the track veers to the left, but it is worth making a slight diversion uphill, to the right, to look at an old limestone quarry, with the remains of a large limekiln. Return to the track and cross a deer fence by a ladderstile or a gate. Go on through another stile.

4. If you feel in need of refreshment, turn left at the next junction and walk downhill, crossing two low stiles to bring you through delightful open woodland to a crossing of paths. Go straight ahead over a rough field and through a tiny car park to reach an entrance to the walled garden of Applecross House. Inside you will find the Potting Shed cafe, which is to be recommended. Retrace your steps through the wood and back to the track taken earlier.

5. Turn left and follow it downhill over a burn to enter the trees again. Go past the entrance track to a house called 'The Kennels', on your left, and 100m further on take a path on the right, signed with an arrow about 0.5m off the ground. This is Roes Walk. It used to run through dense rhododendrons which often formed tunnels, but they have all been removed. Descend the hillside to a hairpin bend, turn left round it and follow the path along by the Allt Beag through mature woodland. Cross an open area and then go on through a beech wood. The burn joins the Applecross River and the path goes on down beside it. Go over a small wooden footbridge and go through a kissing gate onto a

Dunlin

track. Cross this track and go through another gate at the far side. Continue by the river through mixed beech and larch, where you might spot redstarts and flycatchers, and then climb steps to go through a kissing gate onto the road.

6. If time allows, turn right here and cross the bridge to walk 1/4km along the road. Take the second turning on the right, which leads to the old parish church. There are remains of an old chapel in the graveyard, and a big stone with a cross carved on it on the left as you enter the churchyard. There are also two pieces of carved crosses in the church. Behind the large house opposite the church is a Heritage Centre which is well worth a visit. After this pleasing diversion return to cross the bridge and carry on along the road to the beach, where you can walk along the grass behind the sand. Ringed plovers and dunlin feed on the shore and in early summer it is a nursery for eider ducklings. The view across to Skye is excellent.

7. Return to the road again just before the entrance to Applecross House, which you ignore. Cross the burn and a few metres further on notice the spring on the right, which has steps down to it and a metal drinking cup on a chain. Follow the road, with a steep slope on the left, topped with beech trees and lined at the bottom with irises. Continue back to the post office and the car park.

Practicals

Type of walk *Easy walking on good footpaths and roads. The walk passes two cafes and an inn all of which do excellent food.*

Distance: 5½ miles/9km
Time: 2–3 hours
Map: OS Explorer 428/OS Landranger 24

9

Kenmore and Inverbain
– Circuit of Croic-bheinn

Park above Kenmore, GR 754577, where the stalkers' path from Appplecross comes down to the road. Use the wide verge, taking care not to block the passing place. This is reached by the minor road from south of Shieldaig to Applecross via Inverbain, 3 miles, and 3 miles more to Kenmore.

The **Millennium Forest** for Scotland Trust joined forces with the Crofters Commission to celebrate the Millennium by planting broadleaved trees and Scots pine. First a new deer fence over 20km long was erected to exclude the wild red deer population. Then nine separate enclosures were created within the deer free area and over 1.5 million trees were planted. The majority of these were birch as they would have formed the original forest which emerged after the Ice Age. Rowan, common alder, hazel, grey willow, together with Scots pine were also planted.

Beinn Alligin and Liathach from Kenmore

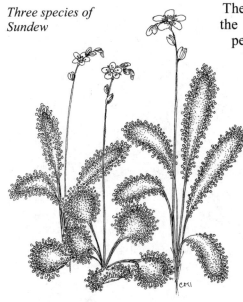

Three species of Sundew

There are three native species of the sundew and all are found in peat bogs and moist hollows such as are traversed on this walk. The round-leaved sundews' crimson tints and sparkling globules of gum give colour and light to their patch of bog. The glands of the plants secrete a clear sticky fluid which detains small insects that crawl over them As the insects wriggle to free themselves the margins of the leaf blades become incurved, trapping the insects. Then begins the process of digesting the soft parts. This gives the plants living in a nitrate-short environment the nitrate they need to make protein for growth. The other two sundews you might spot are the narrow-leaved sundew and the long-leaved sundew.

1. From the parking place go north up the road for a few metres to pass through a gate, on the right, into a field. Strike ahead to join the old path which used to be the only means of access along this part of the coast; at this point it is quite obvious. Turn right and walk downhill towards the village of Kenmore. The path fades, but keep left of a small knoll to go through another gate. Then skirt the edge of a birchwood. The path reappears as a lovely grassy track edged with stones; follow it down to the road. Turn right and walk along in front of the attractive white cottages, with the bay to your left. Enjoy the superb view across the water to Liathach and Beinn Alligin. The road swings left and goes through a wood, with fish farm buildings in among the trees. In spring listen for willow warblers and redpolls.

2. At the top of the road, turn left onto the main road, and follow this round the bay. Beyond a new cottage, selling shellfish and smoked salmon, there is a clump of mature birch trees and here a track, on the left, signed 'bridleway', leaves the road. Follow it downhill to the tree-lined burn, which you cross on a wooden footbridge. The path slants away uphill. Look to your right as you climb for an excellent view of Croic Bheinn and Beinn Bhan. Curve round and up to a low bealach

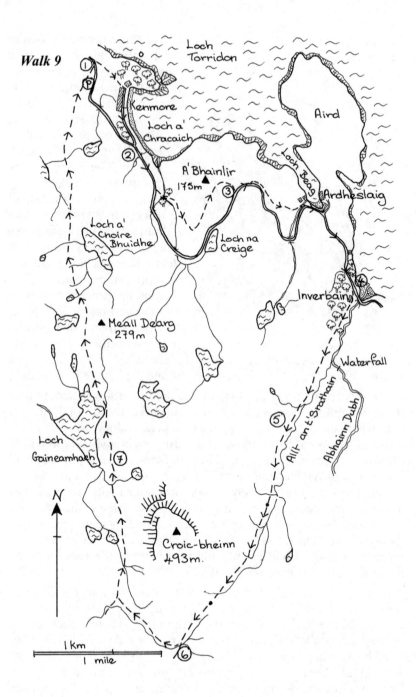

Walk 9

Loch Torridon

Kenmore

Loch a' Chracaich

Aird

Loch Beag

Ardheslaig

A' Bhainlir
175m

Loch a' Choire Bhuidhe

Loch na Creige

Inverbain

▲ Meall Dearg
279m

Waterfall

Allt an t-Srathain

Abhainn Dubh

Loch Gaineamhach

N

Croic-bheinn
493m

1 Km

1 mile

beyond which the whole of Upper Loch Torridon is spread out before you. Descend on the far side.

3. As you approach the road take a small path, to the right, before you reach the loose rock of the embankment. some rock spoil. This brings you up to the road by the end of the crash barrier. Turn left and walk down the road to the first passing place beyond the other end of the crash barrier. Here take a narrow path leading left to rejoin the old path. Turn right and wind on downhill to Ardheslaig. Cross the burn on the new bridge and join the road again. Turn left and follow it as it winds right across a narrow neck of land with crags on both sides to reach the coast once more at Inverbain.

4. Where the road slants downhill to the beach, take a track off to the right signed Applecross (Scottish Rights of Way Society). Go in front of two cottages and on through a gate, the way now a rough stony path through mature birchwood. Look left to see a splendid waterfall on the Abhainn Dubh where it falls into the glen. Cross a minor burn and go on through an area of old shielings, then through a gate in a deer fence, which marks the new Millennium forest.

5. For a short distance the path becomes broad and stony, lined with big rocks – then it vanishes. Cross the boggy field ahead, or circle round the edge if it is too wet. Immediately opposite and beside the main burn, the Allt an t-Strathain, the path reappears above more shielings and climbs steeply up a bank. From here the way to the top of the pass is marked with old lichen-encrusted cairns. The path, however, becomes more wayward and finally disappears into a bog. Choose the best way you can, avoiding the wet parts,and boulders in deep heather, until you reach a substantial cairn at the top of the pass. Here the path suddenly reappears and rapidly becomes good. Enjoy the splendid view down the far side to Applecross and to the mountains of Skye, beyond.

6. After 0.5km further on, at a burn junction, the path forks. A branch goes left over the burn and through a gate in a deer fence and then on down to Applecross. Ignore this route unless you have made arrangements to be picked up there. This walk goes right, along the more obvious branch, which does NOT cross the fence. but descends gently beside a burn until in 1km it joins the Applecross to Kenmore track at a cairn. Turn right and walk on over the moor. In summer its many lochans sparkle blue and beyond is the sea, with distant glimpses of Harris and Lewis. Listen for golden plovers piping plaintively and look for red-throated divers on the lochans. The cliffs of Croic Bheinn tower

to the right – a much more significant hill from this side, it is hardly noticeable on the way up on the other side.

7. The well-made stalkers' track winds in and out around the lochans and hillocks and on past a sandy beach on Loch Gaineamhach (sandy loch). Continue on the path as it descends a sharp slope. Pass through a gate in a sheep fence and stroll on into a plantation. The trees are planted in groups, on turned-over clods of earth, and are mainly birch, rowan and hazel. Just above the road is another gate where you leave the plantation to rejoin your car.

Red-throated Divers

Practicals

Type of walk: *A long, pleasing, challenging walk. The stalkers' path is excellent. The right of way above Inverbain becomes very indistinct near the watershed and is best not attempted in the mist. There is a little walking on roads.*

Distance:	1 miles/18km
Time:	6–7 hours
Map:	OS Explorer 428/OS Landranger 24

10

Shieldaig Peninsula

Park close to the shop at Shieldaig, GR 815540, opposite Shieldaig Island. Or park in a good car park at the north end of the village close to the public toilets, GR 816542. To reach the well signposted village, leave the A896, which by-passes Shieldaig.

Shieldaig Island was bought by the National Trust (NT) in 1970. It was planted with Scots pine 120–130 years ago, possibly by the Fisheries Board (the then owners) to provide poles for fishing nets. DNA analysis of the trees shows that they are not closely related to other Scots pines in the area and most probably came from Speyside. Because the local pines in Glen Shieldaig are of national importance the NT wishes to prevent cross pollination which may affect the stock. To this end they are gradually replacing the trees on the island with trees of local provenance – over the next 100–200 years.

The name **Shieldaig** probably derives from Sild-vik, Norse for Herring Bay, converted to a Gaelic spelling. Herring used to come up Loch Torridon in large numbers but like elsewhere on the coast they don't come any more.

Camas an Leim, Loch Torridon

Walk 10

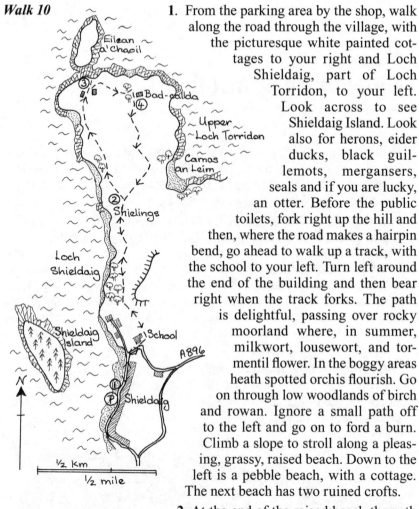

1. From the parking area by the shop, walk along the road through the village, with the picturesque white painted cottages to your right and Loch Shieldaig, part of Loch Torridon, to your left. Look across to see Shieldaig Island. Look also for herons, eider ducks, black guillemots, mergansers, seals and if you are lucky, an otter. Before the public toilets, fork right up the hill and then, where the road makes a hairpin bend, go ahead to walk up a track, with the school to your left. Turn left around the end of the building and then bear right when the track forks. The path is delightful, passing over rocky moorland where, in summer, milkwort, lousewort, and tormentil flower. In the boggy areas heath spotted orchis flourish. Go on through low woodlands of birch and rowan. Ignore a small path off to the left and go on to ford a burn. Climb a slope to stroll along a pleasing, grassy, raised beach. Down to the left is a pebble beach, with a cottage. The next beach has two ruined crofts.

2. At the end of the raised beach the path divides and there is a cairn – note this for your return. Take the left branch and ascend a huge slab of sloping rock, then pick up the path again at the top. The route wanders over a rocky area and then back down to the edge of a low cliff, where you can look down on another pebble beach. Then the way bears right to go past a farm building and comes down to a cottage, which looks out over the narrows between Upper and Lower Loch Torridon. If the tide is flowing or ebbing fast this can be a dramatic place.

3. If the tide is really low, it is worth clambering over the rocks to the tidal island of Eilean a'Chaoil and climbing up to the top. The headland almost opposite is called Rubha na h'Airde Glaise and in days long gone there was a village here, with an inn the ruins of which are still there. Return to the path and cross in front of the cottage, following a line of white painted stones. Scramble up a small rock step onto a flattish area below the top of the hill. Cross this, following a small path as it contours round, and then scramble down a rocky path through a wood to come out on fine smooth grass near another isolated house, Bad-callda.

4. Walk up to the right of the house and cross the moorland behind. Any boggy areas can usually be crossed on stepping stones. Go over a rocky hillock and then down a scrambly rock staircase to the boggy flats above Camas an Leim. Bear right and cross the flat area. keeping to the right side. The path then comes to the cairn noted earlier. Retrace your outward route to Shieldaig.

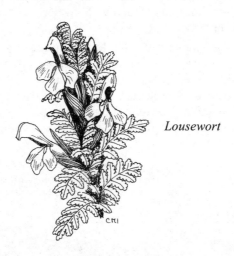

Lousewort

Practicals

Type of walk: *This is a glorious cliff-top walk for a fine day. As you go remember the children, in days gone by, who had to take this route to school, in all kinds of weather, from the croft houses on the headland. Remember the postman too.*

Distance: 3 miles/5km
Time: 2 hours
Map: OS Explorer 433/OS Landranger 24

11

Beinn Damh

Park in the car park of the Ben Damh Hotel (now part of the Loch Torridon Hotel), GR 889542, on the north side of the road about 0.5km west from Annat, at the head of Upper Loch Torridon, on the A896.

Ptarmigan are very well camouflaged and run rather than fly. Listen for their croaking call – like a motorbike! In late May and June they may well have chicks, also brilliantly camouflaged, scuttling after their parents or crouching waiting for danger to pass. As you go look for their cylindrical droppings between the rocks; these will alert you to their presence on the slopes.

On the way up the ridge to the summit the Torridonian red sandstone gives way to **quartzite,** a very pure white sandstone. It was probably laid down 600 millions of years ago, in the shallow sea which then covered north west Scotland. Quartzite gives the summits and eastern slopes of some the higher mountains, their typical white appearance and, being readily broken down by frost action, forms screes.

Beinn Damh looking up Loch Torridon

1. From the hotel car park walk past the hotel buildings to cross a metal bridge. The road then bends right towards Loch Torridon; leave it here and fork left (signed 'Beinn Damh Hill Track') up a narrow path that winds uphill through rhododendrons to reach the main road. Go over the stile and carefully cross the road to walk up a small, unobtrusive, stepped path, on the left, ascending into rhododendrons and pine forest. This soon becomes a well made stalker's path winding up through the trees, along the edge of a gorge through which flows the Allt Coire Roill. It can be heard down below to the left and, as you reach the top of the forest, you catch glimpses of its splendid fall of water through the trees. Beyond this point the forest thins and you come out onto the open moor.

Walk 11

2. Here the path soon divides. Take the right branch and head up into the corrie of Toll Ban, the white hole. Look at the lichens on the rocks, many of which appear to have been painted in amazing colours, with orange, yellow and blue-grey predominating. The path parallels the burn at first but then slants up the steeper side-wall of the corrie to the col between Sgurr na Bana Mhoraire and the other summits of Beinn Damh. The good stalker's path ends and the way continues as a walkers' path, more eroded because it has not been constructed. Go on up to the col, which is the lowest point on the ridge of Beinn Damh.

3. Turn right and walk out over an intervening top to the peak of Sgurr na Bana Mhoraire, from where there is a superb view of Loch Torridon, with Beinn Alligin and Liathach opposite. Perhaps this is your airy perch for a lunch break. Then return over the intervening top to the col and begin the climb up the ridge around the head of Toll Ban. Here look for stag's horn club moss and fir club moss. Look also for the lichen, Iceland moss. As you climb the cairned way the Torridon sandstone gives way to shattered quartzite and walking becomes more difficult. – you should traverse the somewhat unstable boulders with care. At the top there is more vegetation and a small stone shelter. From below this looks to be the highest point, but there is still some distance to go to reach the true summit.

4. Go on down the boulderfield and then up across the next top. From here follow a narrow ridge, which is composed of much more stable quartzite. This ridge leads to the actual summit of the mountain, Spidean Coire an Laoigh, 902m. Its cairn is perched above splendid cliffs on the edge of a steep ridge separating two spectacular corries. The views from here are excellent, including all the hills of the Coulin Forest and further south, as well as the Torridon hills.

5. Return along the narrow ridge. When the angle of the slope on the left, west, becomes shallower, head downwards on a long descending traverse to by-pass the top. This brings you out, once again, on the easy Torridon sandstone slopes above the col. As you go look for ptarmigan. Return down the easy slopes to the col and thence back down the path to your car.

Ptarmigan in summer

Practicals

Type of walk: *A challenging hill walk that is strenuous and demanding. It is only just below Munro height, 902m, compared with 915m for a Munro. All the usual cautions apply.*

Distance:	8 miles/13km
Time:	4–5 hours
Map:	OS Explorer 428/OS Landranger 24

12

Loch Clair and Loch Coulin

Park in a small layby, GR 002582, on the north side of the A 896, Torridon to Kinlochewe road, where there is space for 5–6 cars.

Beinn Eighe, which dominates the view on your return along the west side of Loch Coulin, is a long graceful mountain with fine cone-shaped peaks and a protective shield of quartzite mostly shattered into scree. When the latter catches the sun you will want to reach for your camera and take a whole reel of film. It is possibly even more spectacular when topped with snow. It has two Munros – Ruadh-stac Mor, the highest, and Spidean Coire nan Clach, and its north side is gouged into several spectacular corries facing out over the wilderness of Flowerdale forest.

Liathach from Loch Clair

1. Cross the A-road and continue along the metalled road down towards Coulin Lodge, where a notice says 'no cars, footpath only'. Go over a deer grid in a fence. Cross the timber bridge over the A' Ghairbhe and carry on well above the waters of lovely Loch Clair. The way is fringed

Walk 12

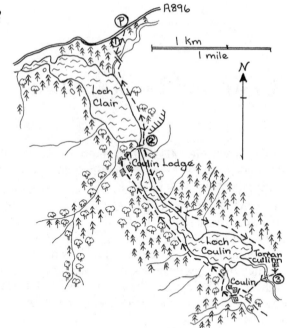

with mature birches, rowans and alders. whilst ahead craggy slopes are covered with Scots pine, as are the opposite banks of the loch.

2. Go on to the end of the loch to a gate beyond the bridge on your right. Take the kissing gate on the left of the gate, where a board reminds walkers to keep to the footpath. Continue on the reinforced track through lovely woodland, with crags to the left, until you reach the remains of a long defunct bridge. Loch Coulin now lies to your right. At a junction of ways take the footpath, going off right, signposted to the Coulin Pass. Go on to pass through a little gate and continue above the loch through a more open area. Carry on through a metal deer gate, into a bleaker area. Here the loch is very reedy. At the right time of the year, look for whooper swans. Cross a small burn and pass a ruin on your left. It is rather desolate at this end of the loch and the path is rough and boggy. Ford the several small burns coming down from the plantation.

3. Take the footbridge over a burn and go by white-painted Torran-cuilinn cottage. Follow the track as it sweeps round to the right to cross the wide bridge over the Coulin River. Go on past Coulin farm. Ignore the path off to the left to the Coulin Pass and press on along

48

the good track as it continues down the other side of Loch Coulin, through birch woodland for much of the way. This is a beautiful part of the walk. Waterlilies and bogbean flourish on the loch and there are mallards on the water. Cross a deer grod and press on straight ahead, avoiding the track which bounds the front lawns of Coulin Lodge, on your right. Pass estate buildings, following the track which swings round to the right and becomes metalled once again. The road passes another cottage and then crosses another deer grid before finally crossing the burn between Lochs Clair and Coulin on a wooden bridge. There is a fine waterfall down the hillside ahead. Turn left with the metalled road and retrace your steps along the side of Loch Clair to return to the parking area, with stunning views of Beinn Eighe ahead and Liathach to the left.

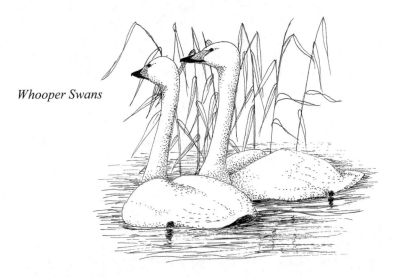

Whooper Swans

Practicals

Type of walk: *On a sunny day, when the air is clear, this is a particularly lovely circuit of two fine lochs, with some of the most superb views in the north west highlands. It is generally easy walking, with one wet area and one short ascent.*

Distance: 6 miles/9.5km
Time: 2–3 hours
Maps: OS Explorer 433/OS Landranger 25

13

Wester Alligin to Diabaig

Park at the junction where the road to Wester Alligin leaves the road along the north shore of Loch Torridon, GR 8332580, or at the cattle grid a short distance further on. To reach this leave the A896, where it starts to makes a large curve, south, at the head of Upper Loch Torridon, and continue along the B-road, through Torridon village. Go on for 8km to take the second left for Wester Alligin.

This is another of **Wester Ross's glorious walks**. The coastal route, taken first, is breathtakingly lovely. To make it into a circular walk the return is along footpaths and the quiet road from Diabaig. To avoid road walking you may wish to use two cars, or, return back along the coast. You could also make use of the post bus from Diabaig to Wester Alligin.

The village of **Diabaig** lies crouched on the shore of Loch Diabaig, an inlet of Loch Torridon. Its cottages are dotted across the slopes of

The jetty at Diabaig

a rocky semi-circle. Loch Torridon is usually described as the most beautiful sea-loch in the Highlands. The hills leaning over it are very old and were so when the Himalayas were thrust into existence.

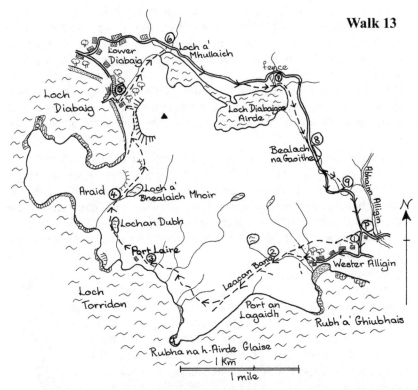

Walk 13

1. Walk down the road into Wester Alligin, turning right at the junction towards the pebbly beach. Go on to the end of the tarmacked road, before Camasdrol, and take the reinforced track leading uphill, on the right. Fifty metres along take, on the right, a small path, sign-posted 'Footpath to Diabaig'. Follow this uphill through lovely deciduous woodland. Cross a small burn and go on to a metal gate, with a sign 'dogs on leads', leading out onto the hill. Beyond towers Beinn Damh. Go on up the hillside to reach a plateau where you join a path coming in, on the right, from above Wester Alligin (in fact, from the parking place where you have parked). Turn left and walk on. At a faint Y-junction of paths take care not to go off, left, round the first headland – this is very pleasant but adds considerably to an already substantial walk.

2. Follow the path over the plateau and on as it contours to the right along the steepening hillside. A small path joins it on the left (this is the one from round the first headland). Then, for a short distance, the sea is directly and very steeply below and it is quite vertiginous. Stand still to enjoy the wonderful views back into Upper Loch Torridon. Soon the distinct path eases continuing, in summer, through a veritable flower garden, and goes on across a low ridge. A less obvious path goes off left here to Rubha na h-Airde Glaise, where there was once a settlement. Continue down the far side of the ridge to cross a valley, then the next rocky ridge and another valley with a burn. Beyond the next ridge the remote white-painted croft house at Port Laire comes into view between huge rocky outcrops. It is only accessible on foot or by boat.

3. Follow the white arrow and path sign painted on a large rock and keep high on the hillside, crossing behind the cottage. Then slant up to a col at the end of this green oasis and go over to Lochan Dubh, the first of two delightful waterlily lochans. Here, in spring, you may find palmate newts and common blue and large red damselflies. Go on along the path as it begins to climb over the brow towards the second loch, lovely Loch a'Bhealaich Mhoir.

4. Climb up the valley side beyond this loch and wind round left over the low bealach. A stunning view down to Loch Diabaig meets you. The loch is an almost circular arm of the sea enclosed in steep gneiss cliffs, with the green fields and trees of Diabaig township at the outer end. Descend the steep path, with care. Then contour and climb up again. Cross a high shelf and then come steeply down, once more, in a pleasantly vegetated wide gully. Where it widens out go between old gateposts and contour round to the right, finally descending through open birch woodland. Look here for wild goats. At a path junction turn left and walk down past the garden fence of No 1. Diabaig. Enter a gravelled area through a metal gate, turn right through a white painted wooden gate and cross the concrete bridge over the

Palmate newt

Allt an Uain into Lower Diabaig. Enjoy the view of the little jetty. (If you are being picked up or joining a second car, there is plenty of parking beyond the jetty.)

5. After enjoying the delightful hamlet, retrace your steps over the burn and up into the woodland, at first following blue 'footpath' signs. Then take the left fork, which keeps beside the burn. Go past a stone byre on your left and cross a tiny tributary to walk alongside the main burn through birch woodland. Continue uphill through a gap in a stone wall and on past a ruined stable with a collapsed corrugated iron roof. Just beyond a ruined croft house, on the left, go through a metal gate in a stone wall and start to climb steeply uphill through open country, with the burn in a gorge well below to your left. After a while the path levels out. Go through a kissing gate in a deer fence.and continue on with the fence on your left, to a metal pontoon bridge over the burn where it flows out from Loch a'Mhullaich. Cross this and follow the shore of the loch, with the fence still on your left. Go through a wooden gate at the end of a little metal jetty in the loch. At the fence corner ford a burn and go up to the road.

6. Turn right, and continue along the road for just over a kilometre, until you see the ruins of sheep pens on the right. Go down the bank and through a deer gate. Then go left through a gap into the pens and wind your way down through them. Turn left to head diagonally down the field, walking below the telegraph wires, towards Loch Diabaigas Airde. Ahead is a waterfall on the Allt Airigh Eachainn and behind it towers Beinn Alligin, with An Ruadh-mheallan just visible above the intervening moorland to the left. The path continues quite clearly across the field until it comes to an old ricketty deer fence, very inconveniently placed right across the middle of it. It is perfectly easy to climb through it, but most people seem to walk down beside it over rather boggy ground to the lochside where it is possible to climb round the end, providing the loch is not too high.

7. Follow one of several paths to ford a burn, just below a telegraph pole. Then rejoin the main path. Once round a bend you come upon a larger burn, the Allt Airigh Eachainn, below its waterfalls. It is not particularly wide and in normal conditions fording it will present no problems. Beyond the burn, the path climbs steadily up the hill, passing through a little rocky defile near to the top, where you emerge onto the road.

Water
Lobelia

53

8. Turn right again and go over the col, the Bealach na Gaoithe (Pass of Winds) and past a small reedy lochan with a wonderful backdrop of Beinn Damh across Loch Torridon. Two hundred metres on take another old path that leaves the road on the left and goes steeply downhill beside a burn. This enables you to avoid a wide sweep of the road. However, if you stay on the road there is a parking area with a good view indicator and picnic tables.

9. The path joins the road again a short distance downhill. Continue down to the cattle grid and the junction for Wester Alligin, where you rejoin your car.

Otters

Practicals
Type of walk: *A long challenging ramble but one of sheer delight.*

Distance: 7 miles/11km
Time: 5 hours
Maps: OS Explorer 433/Landranger 24

Inveralligin to Torridon
– linear walk

Park at the road end at Rechullin, GR 856575. To reach this, take the minor road westwards from Torridon and then the next left turn for Inveralligin and continue to Rechullin.

Corry church serves the communities of Fasag (Torridon) and Inver and Wester Alligin. It was built in the grounds of Torridon House. It is very plain with a simple wood and stone interior and sits athwart a grassy bluff overlooking the sea. On the far extremity stands a solid memorial in the shape of a Celtic cross placed there in gratitude to a past benefactor – sadly the weather has blurred most of the wording.

Bridge at Rechullin, Torridon

1. From the parking area, follow the Scottish Rights of Way sign for Torridon. Stride downhill, towards the shore, to cross a stone-slabbed bridge over a burn. Follow the path as it begins to climb to pass a seat, well placed to enjoy the view down the loch towards Inveralligin. Pass through a deer gate and then on along the cliffs, giving a good vantage point to look for otters.

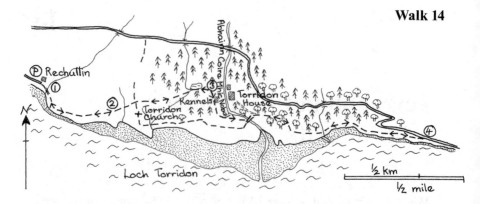

2. Soon the path swings away from the shore and joins the reinforced track from Torridon House. Bear right and right again to pass through a gate in the fence enclosing the little stone Corry church. After a visit, return to the wide track and walk on into the forest.

3. Go through a gate to walk between dwellings and stride on to leave Torridon House on your left. Cross the red-painted metal bridge over the fast-flowing burn, the Abhainn Coire Mhic Nobuil, that comes down from the hills above. Where the track forks, take the right branch and pass between an avenue of sweet-smelling limes. Continue past a beautifully constructed sandstone jetty and onto a metalled track, which comes right to the edge of the sea. Go through a deer gate and on under huge sandstone cliffs rearing upwards. At the end of the track, the narrow road continues to the village of Torridon.

4. You may wish to return once you reach the road. If so, retrace you outward route.

Practicals

Type of walk: *A pleasing coastal walk with glorious sea views.*

Distance:	4 miles/6km (there and back)
Time:	2 hours
Map:	OS Explorer 433/OS Landranger 24

15

Beinn Alligin

Park in the car park on the west side of Abhainn Coire Mhic Nobuil, GR 868576. This is reached by the minor road which branches off the A896 by the Torridon Visitor Centre at Fasag and runs along the north shore of Loch Torridon.

Beinn Alligin, the mountain of beauty, is the western most of the great Torridon tryptych and therefore has a splendid panorama of sea and islands as well of the peaks inland. First reached on this climb is the summit of Tom na Gruagaich, 922m. It is your first Munro of the day and was only added to the Munro Tables in 1996 when they were last revised. Ring ouzels are often seen here. Just below the summit, stop to admire the dramatic gash of Eag Dhubh (the black cleft), and peer down its depths to the corrie floor far below. Sgurr Mhor, 985m, is the highest point on Beinn Alligin and is your second Munro of the day.

Eag Dhubh, Beinn Alligin

The **dotterel**'s favourite haunts are wild barren uplands above 600m where it is most difficult to spot. It is a squat, plump, short-billed plover. It has a white band that divides its grey-brown upper breast from its lovely chestnut and black lower breast. It utters a low plaintive whistle and has a harsh alarm call. It is remarkably tame. The male is duller than the female and courtship is reversed. He does most of the brooding and the rearing of the young. Dotterels are nowhere common in Britain so it is always exciting when you meet it on the broader ridges of some of these mountains.

1. Cross the road and take the muddy, peaty path which starts beside the bridge on the west side of the Abhainn Coire Mhic Nobuil. Follow the path as it strikes off across the moor towards Coir' nan Laogh, the great rock enclosed hollow in the side of Tom na Gruagaich. Cross several small escarpments and pick your way over the boggy ground until you reach the foot of the corrie and the way becomes drier. A clear path climbs

Walk 15

steeply on the bank of the Allt an Glas – the water is beside you for much of the way up, which may be an important consideration on a hot day. Look for starry saxifrage, and admire the water-combed mosses at the burn's edge. Towards the top the corrie bends round to the right and the path becomes much more eroded, so pick your way with care. Early in the summer a snow patch may well be found lingering here.

Dotterel

2. Emerge from the corrie onto a broad stony plateau. If you have time it is well worth walking out left from the top of the corrie when you first reach the plateau – apart from anything else you will have this small summit to yourself because everyone else turns right. Here you might see dotterel. The views are superb. Return to the top of the corrie and continue ahead to the summit of Tom na Gruagaich.

3. Descend the path leading north from the summit, heading for the ridge connecting Tom na Gruagaich with Sgurr Mhor. The way down is quite rocky and scrambly and you will need to use your hands, but it is not difficult, although there is an awkward step down a sandstone slab near the bottom. The ridge at the bottom is quite broad, though precipitous on its east side above the boulder-strewn floor of Toll a'Mhadaidh, the hole of the fox. Look back to see the cliffs of tiered Torridon sandstone forming the north east face of Tom na Gruagaich. Cross over a small rocky knoll, then follow the path up the easy stony slopes of Sgurr Mhor. Just below the summit, stop to be astonished by the dramatic gash of Eag Dhubh.

4. From the summit look down to the Horns (Na Rathanan). They form a splendid narrow castellated ridge; the traverse is not difficult but is rocky and exposed and if you do not like scrambling you may prefer to return by your outward route. Or you may want to return past the huge cleft and down to the first dip. Then strike right down the grassy slopes to arrive in An Reidh-choire below the boulders that cloak the slopes. Here bear left over moorland, continuing around the skirts of the mountain – a long demanding walk, with magnificent views of the sea loch below. Walk on descending gently until you reach a fence stretching ahead across the slopes. Follow this south-east for nearly a mile to just before it turns right, downhill. Pass through the fence, move right to the side of the Na h-Alltan an Donna and follow it down the mountain slopes. Far below you can see the Diabaig to Torridon road. Keep beside the burn as it passes through a gap in the outcrops and continue down to a gate to the road. Turn left to return to the car park.

5. To continue over the Horns, go down steeply but easily to a narrow coll and then begin the scramble. The way is generally obvious, with a well marked path. The ascent of the first horn is steep and the path along the top narrow and airy, but this would only present a problem in high winds or icy conditions. In summer it is an enjoyable scramble. The way off the second horn is steep but wide, and the third is climbed by a scramble up a rock gully. Walk on along the crest to the final small summit and descend steep, rough ground, south-east, to a broad shoulder. From here follow the path to the edge and make your way down over many small rock steps into the corrie below.

6. Join the good stalker's path which comes down the corrie from Bealach a'Chomla below Beinn Dearg. Follow this path to the bridge over the Allt a' Bhealaich and then down the other side of the burn to join the path round the back of Liathach. Cross the Abhainn Coire Mhic Nobuil on another good bridge and carry on down the corrie. The burns are all delightful, a succession of small waterfalls, water slides and deep pools which are a serious temptation on a hot sunny afternoon. Go on the well made path and follow it into a mature pinewood. Here pause to see the substantial waterfall, where the Abhainn Coire Mhic Nobuil falls into a gorge. Carry on to the car park.

Practicals

Type of walk: *Take a whole day to enjoy this long climb and descent. Choose a dry day. Do not attempt in the mist. Boots, waterproofs, map, compass and lots of drinking water on a sunny day are essential.*

Distance:	6½miles/10.5km
Time:	6 hours
Map:	OS Explorer 433/OS Landranger 24

16

Coire Mhic Fhearchair

Park in the car park at Abhainn Coire Mhic Nobuil bridge, GR 868576, and then wait by the bridge for the ten o'clock post bus. This takes you through Torridon to Annat where the bus turns round and continues through Glen Torridon. The bus sets you down at the Coire Dubh National Trust car park, GR 957568, before the bridge over the Allt a'Choire Dhuibh Mhoir. Alternatively two cars could be used.

Coire Mhic Fhearchair, Beinn Eighe

Coire Mhic Fhearchair is Scotland's finest mainland corrie. Find a sheltered corner to enjoy this splendidly wild place in the mountains. Beyond its brooding loch of the same name, rear the triple, pleated sandstone buttresses of Beinn Eighe, to the left the steep scree-strewn side of Ruadh-stac Mhor and to the right the forbidding cliffs of Sail Mhor. Here you will probably see dippers, wheatears and, if lucky, snow buntings.

This is a **long hard walk**, but if you choose a good day, it is an exhilarating, challenging one, which takes you up into spectacular mountain scenery. All the paths are distinct and cairned, and can be wet at times. You will need all your mountain walking equipment – strong boots, waterproofs, map, compass, whistle and high energy food.

1. Take the path that leaves the road on the west side (left) of the burn. The way has been restored extensively in the last few years and all the steep bits are now pitched. It climbs steeply, passing, on the left, Stuc a'Choire Dhuibh Bhig, Liathach's most easterly peak, and, on the right, the screes of Beinn Eighe's, A'Choinneach Mhor. After 2.5km of ascent, cross the burn by large solid stepping stones. Continue onwards for another 1.5km and, just beyond a large cairn, leave the main path and take a cairned path to the right, which edges round below Sail Mhor. As the path climbs, look left to see a string of lochans and beyond a glimpse of Upper Loch Torridon. As you go on admire the watery boulder-strewn wilderness of Flowerdale Forest. Continue climbing along the well defined, path as it begins to drift right, east.

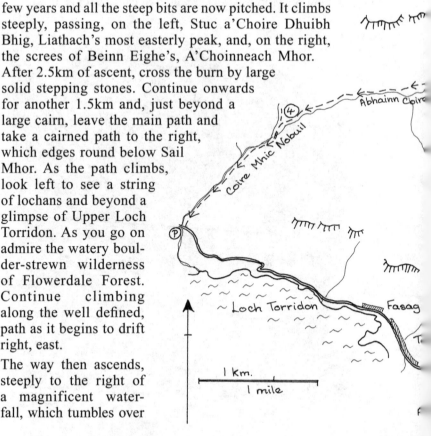

2. The way then ascends, steeply to the right of a magnificent water-fall, which tumbles over

62

sandstone terracing. Sail Mhor towers above on your right. Continue on up and then over the flat slabs at the rim of the dramatic Coire Mhic Fhearchair where you will want to pause.

3. Leave the corrie by your outward route and return to the cairn, where you took the right hand path. Turn right and, for 5km, follow the path parallel with or beside the Abhainn Coire Mhic Nobuil. Restoration work has been done on the path but after rain the peat holds a large volume of water. To the left lies the flaring side of Liathach, with Beinn Dearg to the right.

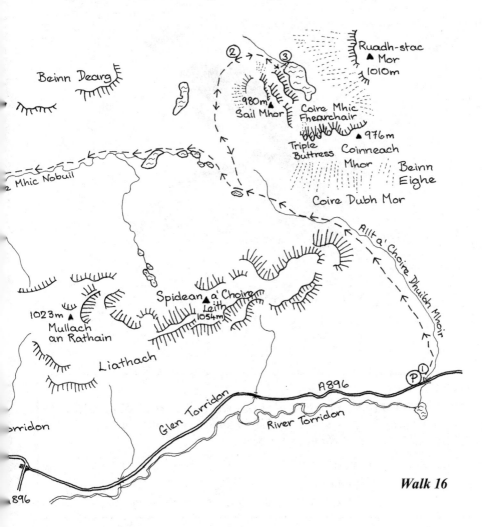

Walk 16

4. Bear left at the junction with the path coming in from Bealach a'Chomhla and continue beside the Allt a Bhealaich. Just beyond the junction of paths is the confluence of the two rivers, the Allt a' Bhealaich and the Abhainn Coire Mhic Nobuil. Cross the bridge and walk on beside the latter. A splendid waterfall tumbles down the far bank adding its water to the main river. Soon the path passes among birch and then through pines to reach the road. The car park lies opposite. Enjoy the view of the Eas Mor waterfall as you cross the bridge.

Snow Bunting

Practicals

Type of walk: *This long walk takes you into some of Wester Ross's most dramatic scenery. Suitable for strong, seasoned walkers. Exhilarating and challenging.*

Distance:	12 miles/19km
Time:	7 hours
Maps:	OS Explorer 433/OS Landranger 19, 24 and 25

17

Gleann Bianasdail and Heights of Kinlochewe

Half a mile east of Kinlochewe, take the turn, north, off the A832, signed for Incheril. Cross the bridge over the river. Continue ahead at the crossroads and go on to the car park, GR 038624, on the left, at the end of the reinforced road. (The land for parking was donated in November 1995.)

This **long, challenging walk** starts as a gentle stroll. It then continues upwards alongside a tumbling river, with many plummeting waterfalls, to go on to where the river leaves Lochan Fada. If the outflow is fast and deep this is where you should return. If you can cross safely, and happily, continue on over rough, boggy but fairly level ground to reach the stalkers' track that will take you back (you could almost dance – if not too tired) easily to Kinlochewe. You may want to make this second part of the walk a 'there and back' on another day, avoiding the river crossings. You could also complete the walk from Incheril car park to Loch Maree and back in an afternoon.

Abhainn an Fhasaigh, Gleann Bianasdail

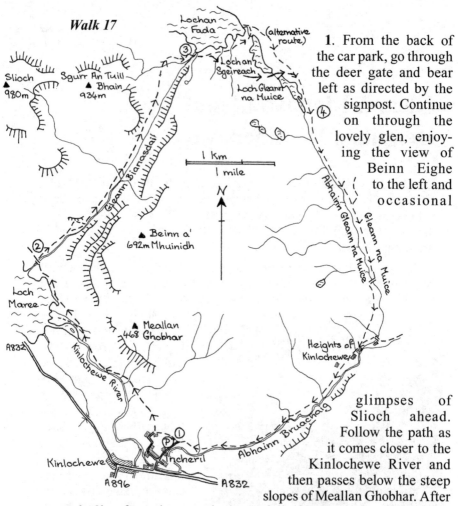

Walk 17

1. From the back of the car park, go through the deer gate and bear left as directed by the signpost. Continue on through the lovely glen, enjoying the view of Beinn Eighe to the left and occasional glimpses of Slioch ahead. Follow the path as it comes closer to the Kinlochewe River and then passes below the steep slopes of Meallan Ghobhar. After nearly 3km from the start, look carefully for the arrow composed of stones and embedded in the grassy sward, directing you, right. This takes you away from the main path. (The main path goes onto an island in the river delta and it is often difficult to cross back to the bank.) Cross a grassy pasture, then pick up the path as it emerges from the river. Follow the delectable way down to the edge of Loch Maree, where you might spot mergansers. Go on through a bank of heather and cross the bridge over the Abhainn an Fhasaigh, the fine tumbling burn that descends, for three miles, through the Bianasdail glen from Lochan Fada to Loch Maree.

2. At the path junction the continuing path goes straight on to Letterewe.

Here, turn right and go on uphill below birch, alder and Scots pine that line the bank of the river, always keeping to the higher path. The way then moves into a wide glen, with the slopes of Slioch to the left and Beinn a'Mhuinidh to the right. Step across the foot of a burn, which has descended in a spectacular fall from Coire na Sleaghaich on Slioch. Go on climbing, leaving the burn far below. Eventually this high level path comes to the top of the ridge and below you can glimpse a corner of Lochan Fada. Then begin the long descent to the lochan. Cross another fast flowing burn, just below another magnificent fall and descend the cairned path to come to the edge of the Abhainn Fhasaigh where it starts its journey to Loch Maree.

3. If the river, 6m wide, shallow and with a stony bottom, is not in spate (when it is dangerous), cross on boulders, or wade, or paddle. If none of these appeal you will want to return by your outward route. But if you have made it across, head on east-south-east across the pathless, flattish, rough 2.5km to reach the stalkers' path to the south of Loch an Sgeireach by passing between this loch and Loch Gleann na Muice.

4. The stalkers' path soon becomes a wider all-terrain vehicle track. Follow this south, through Gleann na Muice and on to the Heights of Kinlochewe. All the way to Incheril the track keeps close to the river. White-topped streams tumble down steep crags and hurry through birch-lined ravines. Stand on the long, wooden footbridge that spans a deep narrow gorge, below Sron Dubh through which, when in spate, the river roars angrily. Go on down, now with the burn to your left, to Incheril and the parking area.

Merganser

Practicals

Type of walk: *A fine, hard walk for seasoned hill walkers. Be prepared to do this walk in two parts if the rivers are in spate.*

Distance:	13 miles/21km
Time:	7–8 hours
Maps:	OS Explorer 433 and 435/OS Landranger 19

18

Mountain Trail, Beinn Eighe Nature Reserve

Park in the car park, grid ref 001650, on the A832, at the side of Loch Maree, 2 miles north-west of Kinlochewe.

The Beinn Eighe National Nature Reservce was the first in Britain. It was bought by the then Nature Conservancy in November 1951 and at the time of writing has recently celebrated its Reserve birthday. It now comprises some 4,800 hectares, from Kinlochewe and Loch Maree, south-west to Coire Dubh Mor between Beinn Eighe and Liathach. It contains several quartzite-topped mountains, high stony plateaux, lochs, rivers and ancient pine and birch woodland. There are many rare and unusual species of plant, bird and mammal which make the reserve their home e.g alpine bearberry, floating bur-reed, dwarf cornel, eagle, buzzard, merlin, pine marten and wild cat. It has always been a centre for research as well as a place to protect a special environment. There is a field station at Ananacaun on Loch Maree.

The trail starts and ends in the car park and is 6.5km long, taking 3–4 hours to complete. In some places the path is steep and rough and walking boots are an essential. Take waterproofs, some high

Beinn Eighe and
Loch allt an Daraich

energy snacks, and some spare clothing. An excellent trail leaflet can be obtained in the car park and at the visitor centre. Keep a close watch on children. Dogs are not allowed on the reserve. The trail was constructed with considerable help from volunteers. Because of its rugged nature, heavy rainfall and the impact of thousands of feet the trail needs regular maintenance. It climbs through different zones of climate, vegetation and wildlife, matching the gradual changes found in nature as you move towards the Poles. The leaflet describes climbing up the trail like a journey towards the Arctic – hence the need for a woolly hat!

Walk 18

1. From the car park, pass under the road. Continue on through birch glades beside the Allt na h-Airidhe, where heather and bracken grow. Follow the path as it ascends through pine and rowan before moving out onto an open area, with stunning views down to Loch Maree. Carry on through more pine and then cross the Alltan Mhic Eoghainn by a stride and look upstream to the waterfall above.

2. Beyond the trees the path zig-zags steeply upwards, the going is hard and you may have to scramble a little. Look for the well placed cairns that help you find the easiest way. Beyond the 300m marker post, the climb goes on over grey-white quartzite bare of vegetation. You need to scramble and climb. In the protective crevices prostrate juniper, both club mosses, crowberry and various sedges grow.

3. At 550m the summit is attained, where there is a huge conservation cairn. Sit out of the wind and count the many mountain tops around you – perhaps some of the 31 Munros that can be seen on a fine day. The

69

cairned route carries on, crossing the plateau below Meall a'Ghiubhais and comes close beside Loch Allt Daraich. After rain small boggy pools form over the flattish ground but the path is stepped with boulders to help you across dryshod. Go on to pass Lunar Loch. It seems aptly described, though it is really named to commemorate man's first landing on the moon. Floating bur-reed grows on the far side. Scattered sparingly over the quartzite lie red sandstone boulders deposited by receding glaciers 10,000 years ago.

4. More well placed boulders help you cross the An t-Allt, which comes down from the slopes above and adds its waters to the Allt na h-Airidhe. From now on the path descends, keeping in sight and sound of the tumultuous burn. There is a good view from here of the Allt na h-Airidhe Gorge and the spider-thread path along the top of the sheer-sided ravine. Go on to cross large sheets of rock crisscrossed with scratches and grooves where glacial sheets moved over them. Again well placed cairns take you across the rough terrain. Follow the path into the forest and cross a tributary stream by boulders.

5. The path now joins the woodland trail just before its conservation cabin. From here follow the marker posts to the car park.

Wild Cat

Practicals

Type of walk: *An exhilarating, exciting walk. The path is well cairned and maintained.*

Distance: 4 miles/6.5km

Time: 3–4 hours

Maps: OS Explorer 433/OS Landranger 19/Mountain trail leaflet

19

Redpoint to Craig

Park in the small car park, GR 731694, close to the view indicator. Or continue on to the end of the road, GR 732687, where there is parking for about 20 cars. To reach these parking areas, take the minor road along the shore of Loch Gairloch, through Shieldaig, Badachro, Port Henderson, Opinan and South Erradale.

This walk needs **careful planning**. You may choose to return by your outward route, some 10½ miles/16.5km in total. Or you may have a good friend who will pick you up from Diabaig – see Practicals. Or you could walk with friends and leave one car at Red Point and the second at Diabaig.

Before you set off it is pleasant to walk out to the stone pedestal set on a rocky outcrop to see the **view**. Below to the left the secluded sands of Red Point Bay provide a warm golden glow. Across the water of the Inner Sound lie the islands of Rona and Raasay, with the island of Skye beyond. From here, too, you might be able to spot Skye's Quiraing, Storr, Cuillin and the flat top of Dun Caan on Raasay.

Fishing station, Redpoint

The sturdy croft house, **Craig**, was built in 1918 as part of Lloyd George's 'homes fit for heroes policy'. Run as a youth hostel from 1935 to 2003, it is now a free bothy run by the Mountain Bothies Association. Inside the house the walls are lined with cedar wood, brought over as ballast from Canada on returning ships. The nearest road is several miles away and when it was a hostel the chest seen in the warden's room, was floated round from Diabaig on a raft.

1. Leave the end of the car park (at the end of the road) by the left of two tracks and follow it down through Redpoint farm. Go across pastures, passing through three kissing gates to reach the grassland behind the shore. Here in the fields look for skylarks, wagtails and stonechats and, on the shore, you might see bar-tailed godwits, oystercatchers, dunlin and ringed plovers. Continue on either along the shore or, on the track, to reach the old fishing station.

2. Carry on along the path between the shore and a fence and then cross the

Walk 19

latter by a stile. Walk on along the clear path through heather and then uphill onto wide sandstone terraces. Press on along the path as it climbs up on the cliffs, crosses several hurrying streams and goes on through some wet areas. It then keeps close to the sea.

3. Dawdle on along the path, fording the streams that race towards the sea and, after 7km from the start of the walk, the Craig

River is reached. Here the path moves inland, keeping well above the surging burn. Scramble over and around huge boulders as the path moves into the birches that line the banks of the peat-stained river. At the right time of the year you might see elvers migrating upstream, creeping through wet moss at the water's edge. Then cross the bridge that carries you over the racing water. It is the latest of many, earlier ones having been washed away when the white water of the swollen burn rose higher than the planks.

4. Once across follow a rather wet and indistinct path that leads uphill to the Craig bothy. Here you may have decided to return by the same route. If you choose to continue to Diabaig, follow the path as it goes uphill behind the building, past a tiny lochan and then over the moorland to the village. The way is much higher and further from the sea than the first part of the walk, but the mountains are nearer and the views spectacular. After 4km the path comes to a deer fence. Go through a gate and walk between the fence and a wall to another gate in the wall on the right. Beyond, join a road and follow it to where it joins the road down to Diabaig. Here turn right. The car park is down by the shore

Elvers migrating up rocks

Practicals

Type of walk: *This is an grand all-day walk and should be saved for a sunny day.*

Distance:	Red Point to Craig return 10½ miles/16.5km Red Point to Diabaig 9 miles/14.5km
Time:	5 hours (4 hours not including time spent driving round to Diabaig)
Map:	OS Explorer 433/OS Landranger 19

20

Old Road from Badachro to South Erradale

Park at Badachro, GR 782738. The parking area is reached by a narrow road that descends from the B8056 towards the shore and the inn.

The **common snipe** is a bird of moor and marsh. It has a long sensitive bill, with which it probes the ooze. It feeds on worms though, in hard weather, insects and some seeds are eaten. The nest is a grass-lined cup, well concealed in rushes, long grass, or, on the moors, cotton grass and ling. When disturbed it dashes into the air with a loud, harsh call and immediately begins a rapid zig-zagging flight. Its display flight (May and June) is very interesting – it descends with its tail outspread and tiny stiff feathers at each edge vibrate rapidly to produce the characteristic throbbing sound called drumming.

Badachro bay

1. Walk back up the narrow road to join the B8056. Turn left and walk on to take a footpath, signed 'South Erradale 5km', on the right, just before a track leading to a barn painted green. Follow this path uphill, crossing a stile, and bear left at a marker post to follow the edge of the higher ground above the barn. Join a track coming in from your left, at another marker post, just before some dilapidated sheep pens on the

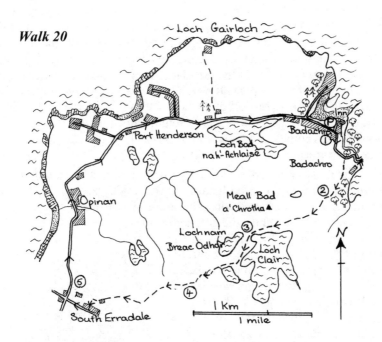

Walk 20

Loch Gairloch

Port Henderson
Loch Bad
na h'-Achlaise

Badachro ①

Badachro

Meall Bad
a'Chrotha ▲

②

Loch nam
Breac Odhar ③

Loch
Clair

⑤

④

South Erradale

1 Km
1 mile

N

right. Stroll on where the track continues above birch, rowan and oak woodland, which lines the slope above Loch Bad a'Chrotha.

2. Fork right at another marker through a gap in the main woodland to your left and an isolated patch of woodland. The track then curves right up onto open hillside. Go on climbing steadily to where you have a good retrospective view, over the loch towards the road to Gairloch and Slioch and further round to the hills of Flowerdale and Shieldaig Forests. Look also for Beinn Alligin – Sgurr Mhor, the Horns and Tom na Gruagaich. The path, now rough, goes on. Ignore all lefts and rights and follow it as it contours, right, round the hill, Meall Bad a'Chrotha, above Loch Clair, which lies to your left. The way is now little more than an animal track as it descends to the northwest corner of Loch Clair, with a marker post to your right.

3. From this point on there is no clear path, and the way becomes boggy. This is not a place to be if the mist comes down, so be prepared to turn back if the weather deteriorates. Turn left to thread between Loch Clair on your left and Lochan nam Breac Odhar to your right, following a wet trod across low-lying marshy ground and up a slight rise to reach a second waymark post above the western arm of Loch Clair. Continue to a third marker and turn right as indicated to pass Lochan Dubh

on your left. At the northwest corner of Lochan Dubh pass a fourth waymark heading on a trod towards three grassy knolls, the left-hand with a prominent boulder visible on the horizon. Your way then bears back left (south) towards the left-hand knoll, weaving left then back right between marker posts through very boggy ground, aiming for a dip in the skyline to the left of the boulder. In this dip the path to South Erradale re-emerges and is easily found. Join it and follow it uphill. Soon the sea comes into view, and then the Outer Isles are visible, with Skye's Trotternish Ridge in the foreground.

4. Step over a stream and walk on up a bank that marks an old culvert. Here you might spot snipe feeding in the muddy areas about the way. Then press on along the route of the old road as it descends the hillside, with the green fields and white houses of the township of South Erradale soon coming into view. The path skirts round the back of a ruined croft, where a marker arrow leads you through a gate and down a track to join a minor road. Turn right and pass through the township of South Erradale to reach the road to Badachro.

5. If you have not been able to arrange a lift back to Badachro you have a choice of either returning by the same route or following the quiet B-road back to where you have parked, perhaps spending some time on the glorious sandy beach at Opinan.

Snipe

Practicals

Type of walk: *This is a challenging moorland walk with a very boggy gap between the start and finish of the old road – which at its best is stony, indistinct and sometimes rough. Do not attempt on a misty day.*

Distance: 3½ miles/5.5km one way
Time: 2 hours one way
Map: OS Explorer 433/OS Landranger 19

21

An Torr and the Badachro River

Park near the outflow of the Badachro River from Loch Bad a'Chrotha, GR 785731. There is room for two cars on the north side of the B-road, to the south-east of the bridge over the river. Alternatively, there is more parking space on the loch side of the B-road, in the direction of the walk. To reach the parking area turn off the A832 at the signposted B8056 for Badachro.

Along the sheltered bays on the south side of the Loch Gairloch lie the villages of Shieldaig, **Badachro,** Port Henderson, Opinan, South Erradale and Redpoint. Badachro and Shieldaig are popular anchorages and the other villages have beaches of red-gold sand, with ever improving views of the Isle of Skye and Raasay. Jetties around Badachro Bay take advantage of the shelter offered by the island of Horrisdale.

Badachro River below An Torr

Walk 21

1. Walk back in the direction of the A-road for about 500m, where a broken rusty iron gate gives access to the hillside on the left. Cross a small burn, on the right, and follow an animal track through the heather and bog myrtle up to the nearest telegraph pole, aiming for the dip between two hillocks. Follow the narrow path as it hugs the higher ground of the right hand hill, which has a prominent boulder on top. On reaching the crest, a fine view of Loch Gairloch unfolds, with the harbour at Charlestown directly ahead. Bear left and follow another animal track, which leads up to a hummock, just left of the next hillock. Pause here and look back at the magnificent mountain panorama of Wester Ross, forming a dramatic backcloth to the reed-fringed Loch Bad a'Chrotha.

2. Contour easily around the hillock to the left on more animal tracks, which lead around the edge of old peat cuttings. Climb to the prominent well made cairn on the summit of An Torr. From here you can see the Badachro River making its short journey from loch to sea and a good view of Badachro bay, with its collection of boats. Leave the little top by one of the many paths to find the easiest way, north, across the bog to the next hill, with a smaller cairn on top. From here you can look down to the jetty at Badachro and the inn. Descend from this hilltop in the direction of the Badachro River to pick up a path which skirts the right hand edge of a boggy area. Look here for traces of cultivation ridges, and a mound at the edge, next to the path, the site of a hut circle.

3. Go on along a very clear path to meet up with another on the bank of the river. Turn right to descend under gnarled birch. Here the burn plunges down over slabs and boulders of Torridonian sandstone between banks covered with oak and rowan. It then cascades in a series of short falls and rapids between sandstone cliffs into a large tranquil pool, with a beach of boulders, before it descends in more rapids towards the sea. Go on into woodland, carpeted with moss and bilberry, to come to an open area of heather-covered hillside where many birch saplings and

a few oak promise future woodland. To the right is a view of the two cairned hills previously climbed.

4. The path re-enters the woodland and leads downhill with, ahead, a view of the island, Eilean Horrisdale. Take care over the tree roots in path, thread through quite tall oak and birch until finally reaching a small rocky stance on the shore. Directly across a deep sea inlet at the mouth of the river are the jetty and the Badachro inn, temptingly close but with a deep swim in between!

5. Retrace the path back up the burn and continue to where you joined it. Go straight ahead here. Take care where the path comes to the edge of the bank that falls steeply into a deep part of the river. Soon the archway of the bridge, next to the parking area, frames the river view. The path then winds left uphill through trees and skirts round the edge of some fallen boulders. It then crosses a gap in a wire and fence post, with its metal gate on the ground, to emerge at the car parking area.

Bilberry

Practicals

Type of walk: *Short but moderately challenging, with fine views – just right for an afternoon's stroll.*

Distance:	2½ miles/4km
Time:	1–2 hours
Maps:	OS Explorer 433/OS Landranger 19

22

The Fairy Lochs

Park in the large parking area GR 806725, just to the west of the entrance to the Shieldaig Lodge Hotel. To reach this, turn off the A832 onto the B8056, signed Badachro and Red Point and drive for two kilometres.

The wreckage seen on the walk is that of a **USAAF Liberator**, which crashed while on its way home at the end of the war in 1945. It was carrying nine crew and six passengers. The plane circled as it descended, looking for a place to land but struck the summit of Slioch before ploughing into the side of the high crags beside the Fairy Lochs. No one survived. On the memorial brass plate, set into a rock face overlooking the pretty pools, are the names of the youthful crew and passengers. This quiet, lovely hollow is a war grave and as such should be respected.

Bridge,
Loch Braigh
Horrisdale

You might spot a **red-throated diver** on the lochs and lochans of this walk. It is a graceful, active, 'playful' bird, sometimes rolling in the water and gambolling. It swims low in the loch often resting its head on its back, its bill pointed towards its tail. When anxious it submerges its body. The adult's head and neck are a soft pale blue-grey, the back ashy-grey, the underparts white,and its throat red. Divers are ungainly on land. Their legs are set so far back on their bodies that they can only waddle, pushing the breast along the ground. This means that they nest right at the water's edge, and so the eggs and young are endangered by flooding.

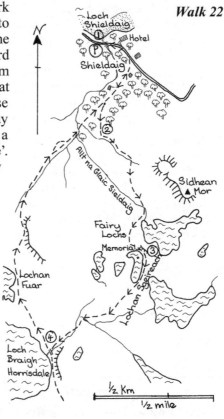

1. Turn right out of the car park and walk back up the road to take the signposted track on the right. Carry on to cross a ford and go on to pass some farm buildings. Ignore the track that goes off right towards a house and carry on the excellent way until you reach a cairn with a signpost marked 'crash site'. Here turn left to walk a narrow path uphill through glades of birch, and then moorland, in the direction of the Fairy Lochs.

2. Follow the small path as it climbs the hillside, contours a short distance and then climbs again. Cross a burn followed by a boggy area and ascend the final rocky slope to come upon a stunning view across to the mountains, Baosbheinn and Beinn Alligin in the foreground, with Beinn Dearg and Liathach through the gaps and mirrored in the first of the lochs below. Descend the path to skirt the west shore of the first loch. It is boggy in places although there are stones in the worst mire and if you felt like adding to them it would be doing other walkers a service. Cross a low ridge at the end of

the loch and then go down the far side towards another lochan, with a third in the distance. In summer these lovely pools support white water lilies, bogbean and water lobelia. As you go on descending, notice a piece of propeller sticking out of the shallow water of the lochan. Opposite this, on the shore, is the plaque on a low cliff.

3. Press on past the wreckage along the path that continues above the lochan, which lies to your right. This part of the walk is not well used and in places it can be very muddy. At the end of the loch begin your descent of the well cairned path. Cross three level boggy areas where the path is unclear and which could make for difficult walking in wet weather. The cairns at the far side are clearly visible so pick your way across to them as best you can. Then descend, with the burn to your left, the clear, stony path. Look ahead for your first glimpse of Loch Braigh Horrisdale, then a wide track which you will eventually join and, finally, an attractive but very rickety bridge, sloping down at an alarming angle. Fortunately there is no need to cross it as there is a shallow ford, beside the bridge, if you wish to make for the lovely sandy beach at the head of the loch.

4. On reaching the track, turn right to walk just above the loch. Follow the way as it leaves the shore and crosses to another small loch – Lochan Fuar, the cold lochan. Then begin the descent towards Shieldaig, following the path at first through pungent bog myrtle and then through delightful birch woodland, with a burn to your right. Carry on to the cairn where you began your ascent to the Fairy Lochs and then continue to the road where you turn left for the car park.

Practicals

Type of walk: *This is a delightful walk but after a rainy spell it can be wet underfoot. Good walking boots required.*

Distance: 3 miles/5km
Time: 2–3 hours
Maps: OS Explorer 433/OS Landranger 19

23

Loch na h-Oidhche

Park in a large area around a corrugated iron shed, at present painted green, on the north side of the A382, at GR 857721

The walk takes you through part of the Gairloch estate, which is creating a **new woodland** for the enjoyment of the present and future generations. By 1998, the estate had planted over a million trees in a thousand hectares of treeless moorland. These are native species, including Scots pine, oak, ash, rowan, alder, birch and holly and all have been grown from locally collected seed. The estate has erected miles of fencing to prevent the young trees being grazed by sheep and deer.

Gneiss, the dour grey rock seen on much of this walk, was formed by the re-crystallisation of still older rocks at various times in the remote geological past, between 2,800 million and 1,400 million years ago. It is an extremely hard rock, producing acid, infertile soil. It is the oldest rock in the British Isles, maybe as old as any in the world. It is great for serious climbing.

Baosbheinn and Loch na h-Oidhche

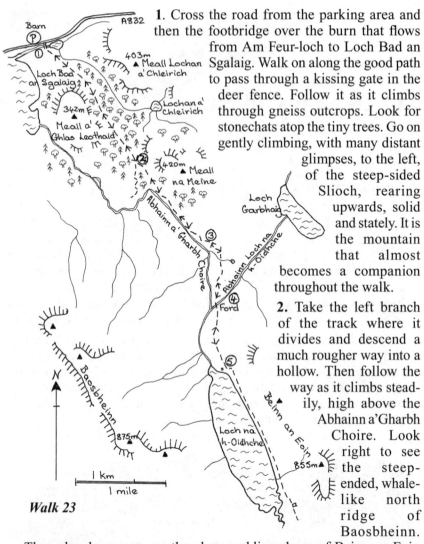

1. Cross the road from the parking area and then the footbridge over the burn that flows from Am Feur-loch to Loch Bad an Sgalaig. Walk on along the good path to pass through a kissing gate in the deer fence. Follow it as it climbs through gneiss outcrops. Look for stonechats atop the tiny trees. Go on gently climbing, with many distant glimpses, to the left, of the steep-sided Slioch, rearing upwards, solid and stately. It is the mountain that almost becomes a companion throughout the walk.

2. Take the left branch of the track where it divides and descend a much rougher way into a hollow. Then follow the way as it climbs steadily, high above the Abhainn a'Gharbh Choire. Look right to see the steep-ended, whale-like north ridge of Baosbheinn.

Walk 23

Then ahead you can see the plum-pudding shape of Beinn an Eoin seeming to plug the head of the glen.

3. Go on ascending the wide stony path as it moves away from the river. Leave the innumerable trees of the as yet miniature forest by the deer gate. Then, as the path continues to climb, Beinn Dearg comes into view. Soon you can see all of Baosbheinn, its summit, corries and long ridge. Notice, on the left, the Torridonian sandstone boulders perched on top of great wedges of gneiss, these erratics left there

by a retreat-
ing glacier or
ice-sheet.

Immature eagle

4. Follow the path to
the edge of Abhainn
Loch na h-Oidhche – one
the two rivers which result soon
after the outflow, from the loch
above, divides. Each one flows
into a different river system. Cross the burn on some rather uneven
stepping stones. If it is in spate, this might present a problem and if
you cannot cross above or below the ford you may have to abandon
your walk to the loch and return. However, when safely across, carry
on up the steepish path to continue across a more level area, pitted
with pools. Then Loch na h-Oidhche comes into view, shimmering
in Wester Ross' lovely light. Its two mountain guardians, Beinn an
Eoin and Baosbheinn, stand proud on either side of the glen. By the
boat shed at the foot of the loch might be the place for a break. Here in
early autumn you can sometimes hear the stags roaring – pleasingly
and almost bell-like – their calls echoing off the walls of Baosbheinn's
corries.

5. Then begin to make your way back. Remember to take care on the
stepping stones. Enjoy the stunning view ahead of An Teallach set
between two nearer, seemingly larger mountains. Watch out for a
golden eagle. Very often you are alerted to its presence by a pair of
irate ravens mobbing it until it moves away from their favourite crag.

Practicals

Type of walk: *A splendid 'there and back' walk taking you into the
lonely slopes below Baosbheinn, the mountain everyone can see
from Gairloch.*

Distance: 8½ miles/13.5km

Time: 4–5 hours

Map: OS Explorer 433/OS Landranger 19

NB. During September and October you should walk only on a
Sunday because of the stag shooting.

24

Tollie Farm to Slattadale

Tollie Farm end – park in a large space, GR 860790, on the west side of the A832.

Slattadale end – park in the car park beside the loch shore, GR 888722, reached by an access track from the A832.

This pleasing route between Tollie farm and the forestry commission car park at Slattadale crosses wild hillocky moorland and comes close to the lovely Loch Maree. It cuts across a huge loop in the A832.

Victoria Falls

The route is magnificently scenic, relatively gentle and generally good underfoot – though after rain it can become rather stream-like! It can be started from either end and if you wish to complete the full 5 miles you should try to use two cars. You might wish to walk half way and return along the same path, saving the second half for another day. Or you could make use of the limited public transport – contact Gairloch TIC, tel 0147822361. This walk starts from the Tollie end. It is easier in this direction and the views are better.

Loch Maree lies in a glacial trough up to 110m deep. It has 66 islands. The larger ones such as Eilean Ruairidh Mor, An Garbh Eilean and Eilean Subhainn contain pristine

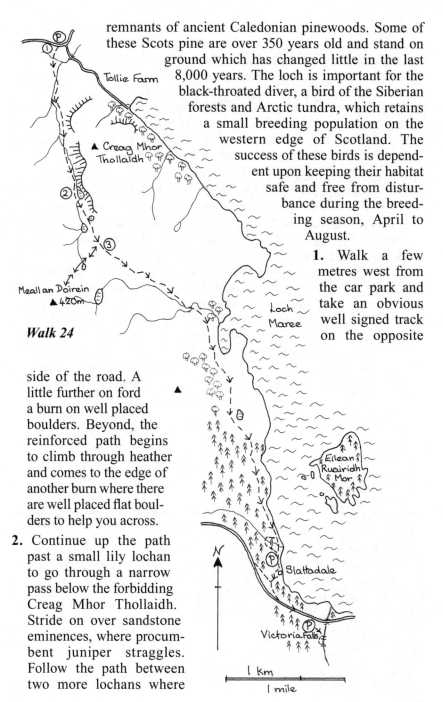

remnants of ancient Caledonian pinewoods. Some of these Scots pine are over 350 years old and stand on ground which has changed little in the last 8,000 years. The loch is important for the black-throated diver, a bird of the Siberian forests and Arctic tundra, which retains a small breeding population on the western edge of Scotland. The success of these birds is dependent upon keeping their habitat safe and free from disturbance during the breeding season, April to August.

1. Walk a few metres west from the car park and take an obvious well signed track on the opposite side of the road. A little further on ford a burn on well placed boulders. Beyond, the reinforced path begins to climb through heather and comes to the edge of another burn where there are well placed flat boulders to help you across.

2. Continue up the path past a small lily lochan to go through a narrow pass below the forbidding Creag Mhor Thollaidh. Stride on over sandstone eminences, where procumbent juniper straggles. Follow the path between two more lochans where

Walk 24

water lily and buckbean flower in the summer. Go on gently descending and then climbing until you reach the watershed where a stunning view of Loch Maree, and its islands clothed in Scots pine, awaits. This lovely, extensive stretch of water continues into the misty distance, it banks lined with trees. Slioch, its head often in the clouds, appears to tower high above all the other enclosing heights. In the far distance you can see the top of Beinn Eighe. From this high point you may wish to make a short, steep but easy scramble, right, to the top of Meall an Doirean. The views from its little summit are superb.

3. The path now leads downward. Towards the bottom of the descent, look for a series of falls where the burn, which has accompanied you downhill, tumbles white-topped over layers and layers of sandstone. Follow the path as it drifts southwards, still descending. Cross another burn and then head on along the path over heather moorland and past a lochan, with Loch Maree beyond. Just before the forest begins, cross a stream that descends through a wooded gorge. Then pass through the kissing gate in the deer fence. Ahead lies a good path through conifers. After a 100m, follow the way as it ascends steeply to a clearing above, from where there is a glorious view of the mountain-girt loch. Then descend steadily to come closer to the loch and from where you can hear the water lapping the shore. Pass through the deer fence and go on. Cross a substantial burn at a ford, or go upstream a few metres to a bridge. The path ends at the large car park and picnic site at Slattadale.

Practicals

Type of walk: *An exhilarating, pleasing walk on a generally good path through fascinating rock formations and across moorland, with some boulder hopping of streams. Spectacular views. You may wish to add another mile to your walk by visiting the nearby stunning Victoria Falls.*

Distance: 5½ miles/9km
Time: 3 hours
Maps: OS Explorers 433 and 434/OS Landranger 19

25

Flowerdale Glen

Park in the car park, on the east side A832, to the north of the (new) bridge at Charlestown and south of Gairloch, GR 810753.

The **'new' bridge** was built in 1986 after the old stone one was damaged during a spate in the river, the Abhainn Ghlas. The stone one gave access to Gairloch from the south when the old single track road used to run between the buildings of the Old Inn and the white cottage opposite the inn. It was built late in the eighteenth century and widened about 1800. The inn was built by the estate around 1792 at a cost of £302.14s. It was given its name because it is the oldest hotel in Gairloch.

The charming **Flowerdale House** was built in 1738 by Janet and Alexander MacKenzie, replacing an earlier house of the MacKenzies, which stood in the field below the road. Close by is the Flowerdale Barn built by Alexander in 1730. On its south wall is a plaque depicting an archer and a lion, together with a Latin inscription and the date.

Barn, Flowerdale House

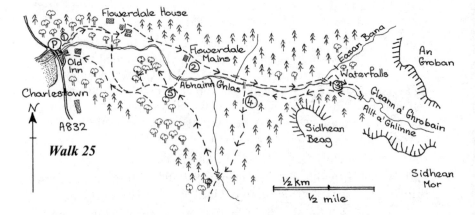

Walk 25

1. From the car park walk into the glen, leaving the stone bridge and the Old Inn on your right. Take the footpath on the right, with the wall and the road to your left. Here enjoy the two man-made lochans where ducks feed and reeds fringe the water. The path leads you back through the wall to the road, where you walk on to pass Flowerdale House. Just beyond, bear right to look at the plaque on the wall of the barn. Return to the road and stroll on. At the track junction, where there is a leaflet holder, wind right to walk a pleasing track through deciduous woodland to eventually reach, on the right, Flowerdale Mains farmhouse and barn. Here, just beyond the gate over the track a notice says that dogs can now be let free.

2. Continue up the red banded good track through scattered trees. To the right, the river hurries down the glen, over its rocky bed. Ignore side turns and continue to where the Easan Bana and the Allt a'Ghlinne join to form the Abhainn Ghlas. Here a bridge, built in 1993 by the army 'for the benefit of the community', takes you across the tumbling water. Pause as you go to see, left, through trees, the Eas Dubh waterfall, elegantly descending in a long white plume.

3. Follow the path as it winds up through Scots pine alongside the Glen Falls, the name referring to the long lonely glen above, which is overlooked by An Groban to the north and Sithean Mor to the south. Go on up steps and out into the glen to cross the burn on another good bridge. This bridge and the continuing path were built by the estate in the year 2000 – the trees here were badly wind-blown so they were cleared at the same time thus creating a new route with superb views to Skye and Longa Island. Walk on along the path to cross a narrow ravine on another bridge, from where you can see both waterfalls. Carry on the

delightful way as it steadily descends to come closer to the river, on your right. Do not cross, but bear left to join a wide forest road.

4. Turn left and gently ascend the gravelled way where the velvety fungus, brown cap, grows in profusion, to pass two blue banded waymarks. Then take a bridge, on the right, over the Allt a'Gharbh Arrigh. Press on along a grassy path, through bracken edged with willow and then follow it as it goes down and down and is well waymarked. Go through young birch where the path can be muddy. Follow the waymarks when they direct you right under several oaks.

5. Join a wide muddy track, close to Flowerdale Mains and turn left. Almost immediately take a faint but waymarked path through bracken to An Torr, a knoll often called Cherry Hill because of the wild cherry trees growing here. From the top the hills that shelter Flowerdale can be seen. Then following the waymarks again, descend the knoll to join the track a little further along. Walk on to join the old road, the way into Gairloch before 1846. Turn right and walk on to a deer gate. Here ignore all gates except for the one ahead. Make sure you avoid the right hand fork and continue with the wall to your right. Go through a hand gate and then past a DIY store. Wind round right and pass in front of the Old Inn. Cross the stone bridge to return to the car park.

Wild Cherry

Practicals

Type of walk: *A pleasing walk through a fine glen. All the paths are well graded and most are reinforced and dry under foot – just one or two muddy places. The return route from the waterfall has recently been put in by the estate.*

Distance: 3½ miles/5.5km

Time: 2½ hours

Map: OS Explorer 433/OS Landranger 19

26

Archaeological trail at Sand

Park in the small quarry car park, GR 762802, reached by the B8021 from Gairloch in the direction of Melvaig. Go past Big Sand caravan site and cross the bridge over the Sand river. After 1.5km take a sharp left hand bend past the old schoolhouse. The signed parking area lies just beyond.

The Sand **archaeological trail** reveals evidence of history, over the last 1500 years, in the field systems, roundhouse sites, rectangular house sites, turf and earth dykes (walls) that stretch across the south facing slopes above the Sand river. The route takes you through heather and bog myrtle from one green area to another, the haunt of stonechats, pipits and wheatears. These grassy flats surround the roundhouses and are found within enclosure walls, suggesting that the Sand valley was once a heavily populated and fertile area possibly right up to the late 19th century. The way is excellently waymarked with jagged Caithness flag stones engraved with an arrow or number – the latter indicating an interesting feature. Try to interpret the remnants of the site for yourself.

Roundhouse remains Sand River

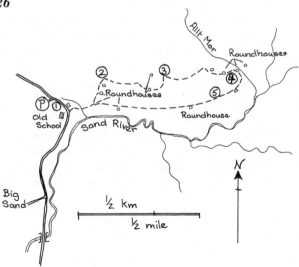

1. Walk back from the parking area to the signposted start opposite a private dwelling, once the old schoolhouse. The trail leaves the road, on the left, passing a ruinous barn belonging to the last schoolmaster, and is site 1 of the trail. Follow the path as it winds down to cross a small burn and up to a gate. Beyond, walk ahead for a few steps and then follow the waymark directing you, left, up the heather slopes. At site 2 you come upon the remains of the first roundhouse, with an outer ring of stones covered with turf. Continue on the well graded path to site 3 where there is evidence of another roundhouse and what is believed to be a rectangular building that may have been built over it at a later date.

2. Carry on up to a huge boulder and then press on along a level path across the hillside, with an ever increasing view of distant mountains. At site 4 look for the remnants of an ancient turf and earth wall. Go through it to a large grassy area. Walk on beside the dyke that would have been high on one side to prevent cattle entering and perhaps trampling a crop of barley. At site 5 you leave the 'pasture' by another turf and stone dyke. Then cross a ditch and carry on towards a knoll. Here you come upon a large circle of rocks.

3. Pass through another field wall to come to site 6, and the boundary of an extensive green field, which you cross. Go on past another round-house and before you descend, as directed by an arrow, climb the knoll

ahead. From it look up the continuing valley to see more bright green, grassy patches among the heather – more evidence of ancient settlements. At no 7 pause to look down on a rectangular house and a roundhouse with a little shieling beside it. At site 8 there is a fine circle of rocks but alas here bracken has invaded the grassy area inside.

4. At site 9 you begin to descend and wind right to begin your return. Pause here awhile to ponder on the extent of the settlement. Envisage the smoke rising from the dwellings and the cattle feeding contentedly. It is easy to imagine children playing about the slopes or would they have had time only for helping with the animals or fetching water from river in the valley below? Almost at the start of your return the path weaves between boulders and becomes indistinct. Here follow the pink arrows painted on the rocks.

5. Soon the flagstone arrowed markers start again and lead you over a large green enclosure. Pass through the remnants of an earth and turf dyke and go on through heather.

After a mirey area you reach another clearing, with another roundhouse. Continue on to the gate. Beyond, bear left to return to the road, where you turn right for the car park.

Meadow Pipit

Practicals

Type of walk: *This is a walk full of interest on generally good paths, well graded and excellently waymarked. Dogs must be kept under close control.*

Distance: 2 miles/3.1km

Time: 2 hours

Maps: OS Explorer 434/OS Landranger 19

Poolewe to Fionn Loch

Park in the car park at Poolewe, GR 859808. If approaching from the south on the A832, you need to turn right immediately after you have crossed the bridge over the River Ewe and it is on your left.

While in Poolewe a visit to **Inverewe Gardens** is well worth while. In the 1860s the land to the east of the head of Loch Ewe was treeless moorland. The change from craggy outcrops projecting from acres of acid peat bog and poor upland pasture to the glory of the gardens was brought about by Osgood Mackenzie. After importing a large quantity of soil he began to create the garden, confident that the warm currents of water, the North Atlantic Drift, would help him fulfil his dream by providing the sub tropical conditions required by rhododendron, eucalyptus, bamboo, palm and other exotic plants. His vision was realised. His daughter continued with her father's work for many years after his death. Almost 100 years after its creation, she gave the garden to the National Trust for Scotland.

Beinn Airigh Charr and Loch Kernsary

1. Return to the A-road, cross and turn right. Walk north through the village using the good footpath on the shore side of the road, from where you have wide views of the bay and from where you can hear

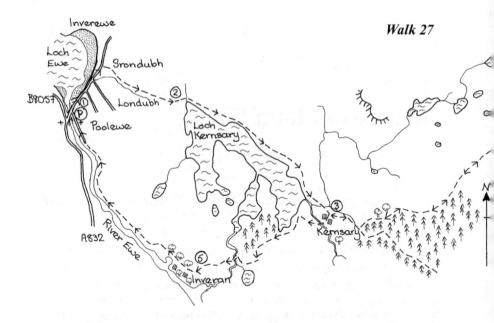

curlews calling. Beyond the last white cottage (Srondubh) on the inland side of the road is a Scottish Rights of Way Society sign to Kernsary. Cross the road, and then the cattle grid beside the cottage, to take the reinforced track on the left just beyond. This almost immediately curves right to go up to a barn, but a good path continues straight ahead, beside the wall. Follow this through a kissing gate in a deer fence into a new plantation – Cnoc na Lise (the Knoll of the Garden). At the end of the plantation go through another tall kissing gate, then out into scattered gorse bushes and then the open moor. Climb steadily and at the brow, look ahead to Kernsary Lodge at the far end of glorious Loch Kernsary. Look back, too, to the houses of Poolewe, picturesquely lining the lovely bay.

2. Follow the clear path down the slope and cross a small stream. The track now rises above the loch, at first very close to the shallow cliff edge, but then rapidly moving away. Step out along the grand way as it passes through birch and a heather garden. From now on the narrow, but clear path continues well above the silvered loch, giving good views of its wooded islands and grassy promontories.

3. At Kernsary, turn left onto a rugged vehicle track. Here begin a steady climb, passing beside a deciduous woodland of oak and willow. Continue climbing, passing through the edge of a conifer plantation,

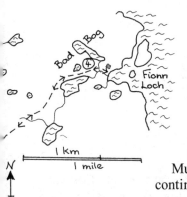

where you might spot goldcrests. At the top of the next slope, the trees are left behind and the track crosses over high moorland, passing Loch na h-Airigh Molaich and Loch an Eilein, before sloping gently down to the boathouse on Fionn Loch. Pause here to enjoy the lovely loch with its tree-clad islands and its surrounding mountains. This is real wilderness. At the head of the loch is A'Mhaighdean (the Maiden), possibly the most remote of the Munros. Beinn Lair to the right has the longest continuous inland cliff in Scotland.

4. Return by the same track to Kernsary Lodge and then go on along the continuing track as it drops down to a bridge over the Allt na Creige. Follow it as it swings to the right, keeping Loch Kernsary to the right. At the top of the slope, begin your descent from the open moorland, with the tip of Loch Maree coming into view. Beyond, the track passes through mixed woodland and then on through birch.

5. Then the track comes close to the wide, shallow River Ewe. Look here for a heron feeding. Continue to the cattle grid where the road becomes public again. and go on to the car park at the end.

Goldcrest

Practicals

Type of walk: *A long pleasing walk to a large remote inland loch, mainly over moorland but with delightful sections through woodland and along a river bank.*

Distance:	10 miles/16km
Time:	5–6 hours
Map:	OS Explorers 434 and 435/OS Landranger 19.

28

Cove to Camustrolvaig and Loch an Draing

Park in the largish parking area, GR 815921, at the end of the road, beyond the township of Cove. To reach this take the B8057 from Poolewe and continue along the eastern side of Loch Ewe.

Above the parking area, on a high craggy outcrop, Rubha nan Sasan, stand a series of **gun emplacements** used to defend the convoys that were marshalled in Loch Ewe during the 1939–45 war.

On 11th September 1998 an **engraved stone** was placed on the crag, among the gun emplacements. The moving memorial says;

> In memory of our shipmates who sailed from Loch Ewe during World War II. They lost their lives in Arctic sea battles on their way to Russia and never returned to this tranquil anchorage. We will always remember them.

Camas Mor

Two and a half miles into the walk you reach another memorial plaque. It bears tribute to the crofters and local services who struggled over the difficult path to help the survivors of the **USS *William H Welch*** that hit the rocks off the Eilean Furadh Mor. The shipwreck occurred during icy weather and a snow storm on the night of February 26, 1944. Of the crew of 74 only 12 survived. Two ladies from Cove, Mrs Katrina Kennedy and Mrs Jean McKenzie, are remembered on the plaque. They struggled to the scene carrying large jugs of tea, food, blankets, and candles to light fires to warm and revive the survivors. Alfred MacKinnon is also mentioned. He carried an oil covered survivor on his back over the rough path.

Walk 28

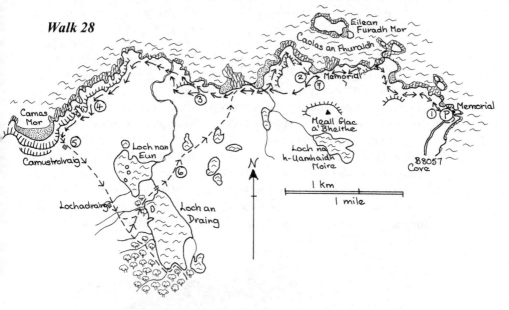

1. Go through the kissing gate at the far end of the car park and walk ahead, stepping across large clumps of turf, avoiding the water between. Then skirt the bay to pick up a path climbing above it. Avoid the peat diggings and go on ascending gently, listening for curlews calling from the shore as you go. Continue on choosing the path, from several, that keeps just above the huge slabs of sandstone high above the shore. Wind round a large, deep inlet, where the sea turns to dark blue. Go round the next bay and follow the driest of several paths. Look across the loch to see the sands of Slaggan, bright gold in the sunlight and also to see the houses of

Mellon Charles, with An Teallach and Coigach in the distance. Cut across the next small headland, with the very green island of Eilean Furadh Mor across right. Carry on to come to a plaque, detailing the shipwreck, and a seat to sit and ponder on the scene. On the shore, beyond, lie the rusting hulks of two lifeboats, unused on the night of the disaster.

2. Follow the shore path and after 300m move inland for a very short distance. Then keep to the sea side of the hillock. Go on, using good animal tracks, keeping close to the shore or the cliff edge to avoid the inland moorland of peat hags. Look out to sea to spot the Isle of Lewis and the mountains of Harris, with the Shiant islands in front. Descend towards a storm beach and make your way over the boulders or, just behind them, on a strip of grass. Cross a small stream on boulders or use a little bridge upstream. Then take a path behind the storm beach and to the right of a sheep pen constructed of cobbles. Continue round the bay on a good sheep walk and at the far end climb up off the shore and walk along the edge of the peaty moorland. Here look for evidence of otters, bright green mounds close to small pools beneath rocks – green because they are well fertilised by spraints (droppings). Keep well up between the edge of the peat and the cliff edge. If the trod disappears temporarily continue on and it will soon reappear.

3. Pass to the inland side of a hillock. Cross the next burn, where you might have to move upstream to find an easier place to cross. Don't forget to return to pick up the good sheep track. Wind round the next

Curlew

bay on the high level rim of the cliffs and, half way along, descend a green gully to continue on a grassy way – as the sheep do. As you near an immensely deep and sheer sea inlet, climb the easy slope, left, in good time, through heather and crowberry and cross where the chasm is shallow. Carry on towards a post on a small hillock. From here you can see that the cliff around the next bay is very high, but still the good sheep trod takes you safely round. For much of the rest of the walk it takes you along a broad ledge above the cliff but below the bog.

4. At the next inlet, head inland along a good trod and stay with it where it takes you behind several low hillocks between which you can glimpse the sea. Ahead is a long forbidding ridge ending in very high cliffs. Below the ridge is a bothy and this is where you are aiming. But first there is another bay to wind round where a steep path takes you down to a gully to be able to circumnavigate the next chasm. This brings you to an old turf dyke on the cliff edge, where it is safer to walk on the land side. Look over with care at the glorious silver sand bay of Camas Mor far below. This is reached by a steep zig zag path, which has to be re-ascended and is not attempted on this walk, Carry on slightly inland to the abandoned croft of Camustrolvaig, now an intriguing shepherd's bothy.

5. By the building join the rough Inverasdale track and stride along it for about a mile, with a wonderful view of the mountains of Wester Ross. Go past the ruined croft house of Lochadraing, where there is a stile on the left, which you ignore. Stroll on, beside the sheep fence to take the next stile over it. Look half left to see a widish path climbing a hillock and head across the pasture to reach it. Continue along the way as it passes through a glorious arch of birch. The pleasing track goes on alongside Loch an Draing to cross a charming footbridge over the burn that flows from it into Loch nan Eun. These two lochs lie in a channel formed by the Loch Maree fault which bisects the peninsula. Climb the stile beside a gate and head on along the track that crosses peaty moorland.

6. Suddenly the good track ends in a very boggy area. Look half left to see the faint outline of where it continues – under water. Cross a wide stream and then make you way as best you can along the line of the track to a rocky outcrop. Here the track emerges, winds round the protuberance and becomes a delight to walk beside Lochan Clais an Fhraoich. Press on the gently climbing way over the bracken and heather moorland. Pass a lochan on your right and then the track descends and ends in a boggy area, just above the storm beach, crossed earlier. Here bear right on a sheep trod to walk behind the the 'wall'

of boulders. Cross the little bridge over the burn and climb to the left of a hillock with the green island away to the left. Go on to retrace your outward route to reach the seat by the memorial plaque to the shipwreck.

7. Return over the two and a half miles taken at the outset of the walk to arrive at the car park with, hopefully, enough energy to left to climb the crag with the gun emplacements and the memorial.

Redshanks feeding

Practicals

Type of walk: *Exhilarating and suitable for hardy walkers capable of covering the 10–11 miles over some very challenging terrain. Some walkers will wish to visit the memorial to the shipwreck and prefer to return from there (5 miles).*

Distance: 10–11 miles/17km or 5 miles/8km

Time: 5–6 hours or 2–3 hours

Maps: OS Explorer 434/OS Landranger 19

29

Mellon Udrigle

Park in the large sandy car park beyond the camp site and behind the sand dunes on the right of the road, GR 890959. To reach this leave the A832 at Laide, at the south end of Gruinard Bay, and take the minor road which carries on round the bay, signed Mellon Udrigle and Opinan.

The **Great Skua** is a large, heavily built bird, dark brown in colour, with a large white patch on its outspread wings. It has an aimless, drifting flight until it spots a flock of gulls harrying a shoal of fish. Its flight then becomes powerful and direct as it singles out its luckless victim and harasses it until it disgorges a half digested meal or the fish it has just caught.

The bay at Mellon Udrigle

1. From the car park walk down beside the burn to the delightful white sand beach. Cross the burn and go round the top of the beach, heading west. Enjoy the superb views across the bay to Coigach, and further

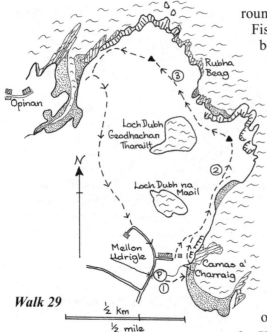

Opinan

Rubha Beag

③

Loch Dubh Geodhachan Tharailt

N

Loch Dubh na Maoil

②

Mellon Udrigle

Camas a' Charraig

P

①

Walk 29

½ km

½ mile

round to An Teallach and the Fisherfield hills. From the beach skirt the Old School, the last house before the shore, on its seaward side to join a grassy path rising along the top of the low cliffs. It soon becomes a wide grassy track heading for the hill directly in front of you – there are many paths wandering off to the right, which you might wish to explore if you have lots of time. The coast here is delightful and you should see seals, divers, gannets and fulmars, and with luck, otters.

2. Climb the low hill, taking the left branch where the track divides and making for the cairn on the top. Continue down the track to cross the next bay, between the sea and a freshwater loch. The path becomes indistinct in boggy ground on the far side, but make for the top of the next hill where the way reappears as you climb the slope. At the cairned top, pause to admire the extensive view of Gruinard Bay.

3. Head on towards the next cairn across an area of peat hags where the wet area can mostly be avoided by keeping to the highest ground. This hill overlooks the sandy, island-studded bay below Opinan. Make your way down towards the settlement over short heather and rock slabs and join one of several paths all going in the same direction. They gradually converge to join a substantial track leading back round the side of the hills and over moorland to Mellon Udrigle. Here in season great skuas fly past and curlews call. The track curves round to the left

Bog Bean

and joins the road coming up from a new bungalow. Follow the route to cross a tiny bridge and return to the car park.

Thrift

Great Skuas

Practicals

Type of walk: *Short, easy and with lovely views.*

Distance: 2 miles/3.4km
Time: 1–2 hours
Map: OS Explorer 434/OS Landranger 19

30

Inverianvie and Gruinard Rivers

Park in the large car park across the road from the sandy beach of Gruinard Bay, GR 952899, reached by the A832 from Gairloch to Braemore Junction.

Gruinard Island, belonging to the Gruinard Estate, lies two miles offshore from the car park. In the early days of the 1939-45 war the island was compulsory purchased to be used as a testing ground for the effect of a biological toxin – anthrax. Sheep were tethered and, next day after a phial of the anthrax 'soup' was detonated, they began to die. Then a Wellington bomber was used to drop a small bomb on the island containing more anthrax. Again all the animals died quickly but the spores survived. Spores of anthrax have a 'shelf-life' in the soil of 100s of years. Eventually in 1987 the island was sprayed with formaldehyde and in 1990 the island was given the all clear. In September 2002 two

Gruinard River

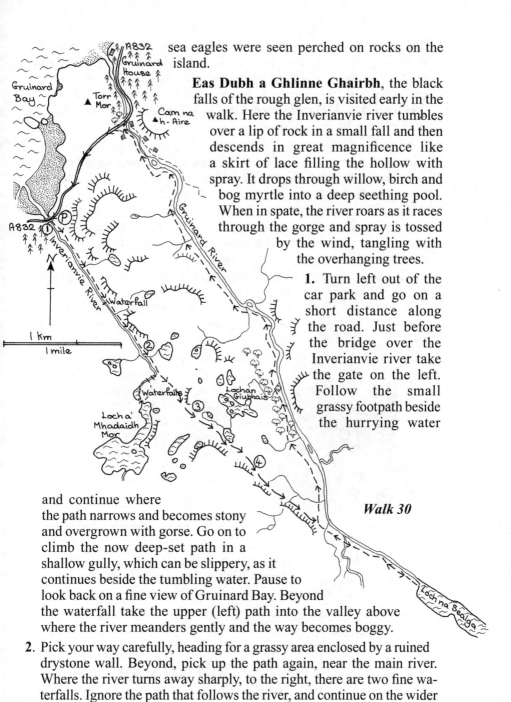

sea eagles were seen perched on rocks on the island.

Eas Dubh a Ghlinne Ghairbh, the black falls of the rough glen, is visited early in the walk. Here the Inverianvie river tumbles over a lip of rock in a small fall and then descends in great magnificence like a skirt of lace filling the hollow with spray. It drops through willow, birch and bog myrtle into a deep seething pool. When in spate, the river roars as it races through the gorge and spray is tossed by the wind, tangling with the overhanging trees.

1. Turn left out of the car park and go on a short distance along the road. Just before the bridge over the Inverianvie river take the gate on the left. Follow the small grassy footpath beside the hurrying water and continue where the path narrows and becomes stony and overgrown with gorse. Go on to climb the now deep-set path in a shallow gully, which can be slippery, as it continues beside the tumbling water. Pause to look back on a fine view of Gruinard Bay. Beyond the waterfall take the upper (left) path into the valley above where the river meanders gently and the way becomes boggy.

Walk 30

2. Pick your way carefully, heading for a grassy area enclosed by a ruined drystone wall. Beyond, pick up the path again, near the main river. Where the river turns away sharply, to the right, there are two fine waterfalls. Ignore the path that follows the river, and continue on the wider

path, heading for the saddle in the small ridge ahead. Just before the ridge the path swings left to avoid a marshy area. Go on along the path until it starts to climb. Here cut off right, passing below a line of small crags and then climb diagonally up the slope to reach the col, where you are rewarded with a superb view, south-east, towards An Teallach, Beinn Dearg Bheag and the other Fisherfield mountains beyond.

3. Head gently downhill towards two small lochans where, in late spring, you might spot a cuckoo, and then continue to the right of the pools to cross the shoulder of a small hill. Follow round the shore to the top end of the second, larger lochan – pretty with bogbean in the summer – and walk up the obvious small valley, which leads away from it. As you near the col it can be very wet but the worst can be avoided by going a short way up the ridge. The view of An Teallach from here is even more magnificent as it towers above Loch na Sealga.

4. Head down across the hillside, keeping the line of cliffs to your right. Look ahead to see the Gruinard River and the track beside it. The cliff line leads straight to the track down an easy slope. On reaching the track, turn right to visit Loch na Sealga, or left, to head back on the good vehicle track to Gruinard Bay. At the end of the track go through a gate and bear left to the A-road. Turn left to walk for a mile to return to the parking area. This can be a busy road, so walk with care, using the grassy verges especially the one on the right hand side which is wider.

Sea Eagle

Practicals

Type of walk: *This is a challenging, dramatic walk into the wild moorland above several fine waterfalls. Use a map and carry a compass when you cross from one river to the other.*

Distance: 8 miles/13km or 10 miles/16.5km if you visit Loch na Sealga

Time: 4 hours or 5 hours

Map: OS Explorer 434 and 435/OS Landranger 19

NB. Avoid this walk during the stalking season

31

Badrallach to Scoraig

Park at the end of the road, in a small parking area, GR 055919, beyond the cottages at Badrallach. To reach this drive south-east from Dundonell along the A832 for two miles. Take the left turn, signed 'Badrallach, 8½ miles', and drive along the single-track road, with passing places. Once beyond the hairpin bend, the road drops steeply down to the scattered cottages that make up the settlement.

There is no road to **Scoraig**. A five mile path is passable to walkers and a few brave mountain bikers. It is well maintained as it is the only way out of the peninsula by land. Some people cross Little Loch Broom, by boat, to reach the mainland. This was the way the secondary school children journeyed to Ullapool as weekly boarders before their school was built by parents. For some years it was closed because of the lack of children, but is now open again and, at the end of 2010, had sixteen pupils.

Beinn Ghobhlach from Scoraig

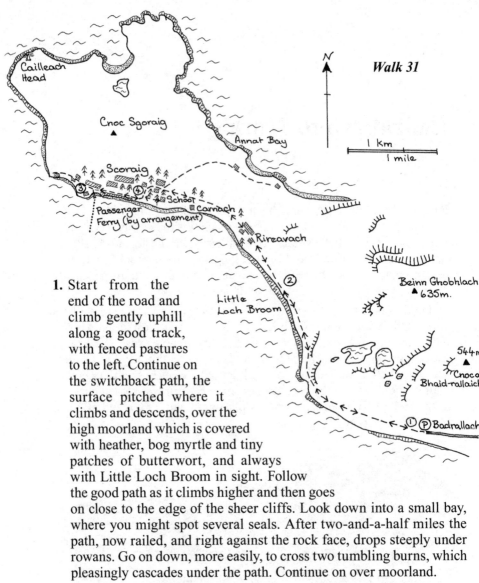

Walk 31

1. Start from the
end of the road and
climb gently uphill
along a good track,
with fenced pastures
to the left. Continue on
the switchback path, the
surface pitched where it
climbs and descends, over the
high moorland which is covered
with heather, bog myrtle and tiny
patches of butterwort, and always
with Little Loch Broom in sight. Follow
the good path as it climbs higher and then goes
on close to the edge of the sheer cliffs. Look down into a small bay,
where you might spot several seals. After two-and-a-half miles the
path, now railed, and right against the rock face, drops steeply under
rowans. Go on down, more easily, to cross two tumbling burns, which
pleasingly cascades under the path. Continue on over moorland.

2. Pass through a gate in the deer fence and carry on along a track. To
the left the first dwelling of the peninsula lies hidden in a planting
of conifers. Nearby is a windmill for producing its electricity. Go on
through the settlement of Rireavach. Here some of the ruins of the
old crofthouses have been turned into dwellings, each with its own
unobtrusive windmill. Above these dwellings are a few widely spaced
houses, mostly hidden by trees, which act as windbreaks. Ignore the

right turn over the hill and go on to pass Scoraig secondary school and take the next turn left to follow a track down towards the loch. Head on as it turns right, with haymeadows to the right, to come to the jetty and several more dwellings and windmills – these are made on the peninsula.

3. Look across the loch to Badluarach. On Mondays, Wednesdays and Fridays, at the time of writing, a small boat with an outboard motor, collects the post for the Scoraig peninsula. It leaves mid-morning and sometimes walkers can go with it to start their walk from the jetty. The post office at Durnamuck will give you the details and you must telephone in advance to see if it is available (01854-633208) – but remember you will need to be met at Badrallach if you wish to avoid the 8½ mile walk to the A832. Then start your return. From the jetty, bear right to climb steps up a grassy slope and follow the track as it winds right. Continue along the pleasing way, walked earlier, with the loch to the right. Ignore the left turn and go on ahead past some wooden sheep pens. Take a gated path to walk beside conifers and over a pasture to a stile to the primary school.

Butterwort

4. Return to the main track and take the right turn, ignored just before, and follow it as it bears right to pass the secondary school once more. Then start your return with a splendid view of Beinn Ghoblach, Sail Mhor and more of An Teallach's imposing mass ahead of you.

Practicals

Type of walk: *This is another of Wester Ross's hidden gems – along high cliffs, over wild moorland, always within sight of the sea loch and as an extra bonus – good dry paths.*

Distance: 5½ miles/9km one way

Time: 3 hours one way

Maps: OS Explorer 435/OS Landranger 19

32

Corrie Toll an Lochain

Park in the car park at Corrie Hallie on the A832, GR 114851 about 4km south-east of Dundonnell Hotel. This is very popular with people going to the bothy or climbing An Teallach. Try to get there early. Do not use the parking for the Corrie Hallie shop.

An Teallach (the forge) is one of the finest of Scotland's mountains. The famous view of it is from Destitution Road – built during the potato famine to provide employment – over the high ground between Braemore Junction and Dundonnell. It is largely composed of Torridon sandstone which gives it its reddish colour, but the eastern spurs are capped with Cambrian Quartzite. It has two Munros, Sgurr Fiona, 1059m, and Bidein a'Ghlas Thuill, 1062m. Sgurr Fiona and its magnificent outlying pinnacled ridge, Corrag Bhuidhe, enclose Coire Toll an Lochain.

Coire Toll an Lochain

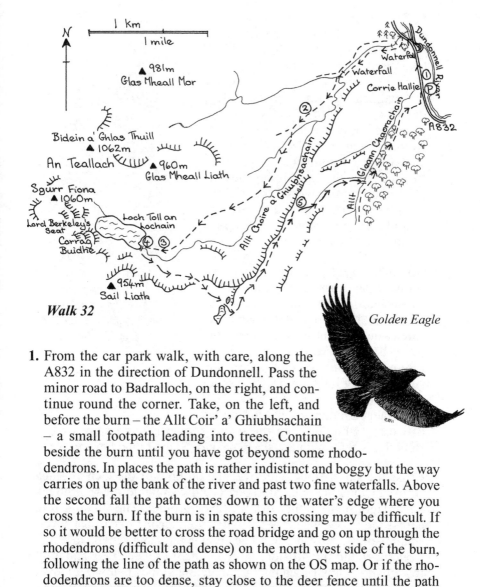

Walk 32

Golden Eagle

1. From the car park walk, with care, along the
   A832 in the direction of Dundonnell. Pass the
   minor road to Badralloch, on the right, and continue round the corner. Take, on the left, and
   before the burn – the Allt Coir' a' Ghiubhsachain
   – a small footpath leading into trees. Continue
   beside the burn until you have got beyond some rhododendrons. In places the path is rather indistinct and boggy but the way
   carries on up the bank of the river and past two fine waterfalls. Above
   the second fall the path comes down to the water's edge where you
   cross the burn. If the burn is in spate this crossing may be difficult. If
   so it would be better to cross the road bridge and go on up through the
   rhodendrons (difficult and dense) on the north west side of the burn,
   following the line of the path as shown on the OS map. Or if the rhododendrons are too dense, stay close to the deer fence until the path
   becomes clear and then walk on by the river. Just before the second
   waterfall, cross the stile over a fence. Ignore an obvious right branch
   following a tributary, and continue left by the main river to the next
   waterfall. Here the two paths join.

2. Follow the path as it leaves the river-side and cuts off along the north-west edge of the ridge. At a substantial fork take the left branch (the right branch goes up onto the ridge heading for An Teallach). Continue up the valley; in places the path is indistinct, but soon becomes clear and well cairned. Notice the spectacular meanders in the burn at one point close to the path. Beyond these the path climbs the hill-side on a rising traverse, leaving the burn below. Then the path contours roughly before going steeply uphill again.

3. Go round the lip of the corrie and across a flat grassy area to Loch Toll an Lochain. Coire Toll an Lochain is rightly held to be one of the two finest corries on the Scottish mainland – the other is Coire Mhic Fhearchair on Beinn Eighe, see Walk 16. Above the still waters of the loch rises the spectacular rock scenery of An Teallach – the jagged pinnacles and buttresses

Bog Asphodel and
Sphagnum

of Corrag Bhuidhe, and the leaning, overhanging spire of Lord Berkeley's seat, with the sharp peak of Sgurr Fiona beyond.

4. Cross the small stone dam over the outflow of the loch and head across the bog beyond, taking care and keeping to the right to take advantage of the rather drier, higher ground. Then pick a route across the rocky, heathery ground beyond, using one of the several small paths which cross it, all heading in the same general direction. Contour round the hillside, through small broken crags and go on towards two small lochans on the gentle slopes below Sail Liath. Stride on between the two lochans and round the right hand end of a line of low crags. Bear leftish and set off down the ridge, following a good clear path along the ridge crest. Enjoy this splendid high level walkway above sloping quartzite slabs. Here you might see ravens, soaring and wheeling, revelling in their mastery of the air.

5. After about 1km, head away from the ridge top path, turning right down into Gleann Chaorachain, with the beginnings of a small burn on your right. Cross the burn and carry on down its south bank over steepish grass and heather until it joins the Allt Gleann Chaorachain. Cross the bridge just upstream from the confluence and climb up the far side through open birch woods to join the main track from Shenavall to Corrie Hallie, see Walk 33. Turn left and go down the track to pass through a gate. Continue down to the parking area.

Large Red Damselfly

Ravens

Practicals

Type of walk: *Another challenging walk that takes you into the lower slopes of An Teallach, where boots, good waterproofs, a map and a compass are essentials.*

Distance: 6½ miles/10.6km
Time: 5 hours
Map: OS Explorer 435/OS Landranger 19

33

Corrie Hallie to Shenavall

Park on the A 832, about 4km south of Dundonnell, GR 114851.See parking note for walk 32.

Volunteers of the Mountain Bothies Association maintain old cottages to provide basic shelter in remote places for walkers and climbers. **Shenavall bothy** is possibly the most popular one in Scotland. The accommodation is basic but the roof and floor are sound and there are fireplaces. Anyone can use the bothy but it must be left clean and tidy. It is a good base for those climbing the six Fisherfield Munros, and its situation is superb, with the wide strath in front and Beinn a'Chlaidheimh and Beinn Dearg Mor soaring dramatically opposite.

Shenavall and Beinn Dearg Mor

These two mountains, in the **Fisherfield Forest**, can be seen in all their dramatic glory from Shenavall. Fisherfield Forest (or The Whitbread Wilderness) was long owned by the redoubtable Colonel Whitbread of brewing fame, who guarded it jealously against intrusion. Except during the stalking season he reluctantly tolerated walkers and climbers on their way to ascend the six Munros found here. The area was notorious for the inaccuracy of the Ordnance Survey map – apparently the mappers were allowed into the forest only for the minimum possible time and they had to work in appalling weather. This resulted in several contours being missed off the tops of A'Mhaighdean, Ruadh Stac Mor and Beinn a'Chlaidheimh so they were late additions to the Munro Tables. Various spectacular cliffs were also missed. Fortunately this has now been put right.

Grey Wagtails

1. Cross the road from the parking area and go up the reinforced track opposite. It zigzags and comes to a gate. Go through and follow the track through pastures and into delightful birch woodland, with the burn, the Allt Gleann Chaorachain, down below to the right. Beyond the hurrying water, great slabs of rock (quartzite) slope upwards, with lines of thin vegetation, and behind it all towers An Teallach.

2. Once through the trees, cross the burn at a shallow ford or carry on for 100m to a recent (but somewhat insecure-looking) bridge. Look for the fine waterfall in a cleft to the left. Follow the track as it winds up the right side of the glen and out onto the moor above. Below, on the left, is Loch Coire Chaorachain, the source of the waterfall. To the right is the long rocky climb up to Sail Liath, an outlier of An Teallach.

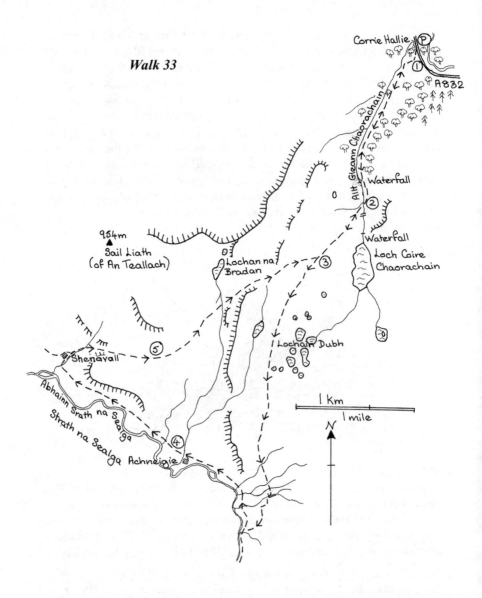

Walk 33

Corrie Hallie

A832

Waterfall

Waterfall

Loch Coire
Chaorachain

954m
Sail Liath
(of An Teallach)

Lochan na
Bradan

Lochan Dubh

Allt Gleann Chaorachain

Shenavall

Abhainn Srath na Sealga

Strath na Sealga   Achneigie

1 Km
1 mile
N

3. Carry on to a cairn. Here, ignore the path that leaves the main track, right, and go on along the rocky track as it crosses the high moor. Ahead, dominating the view, is the sharp cone of Beinn a'Chlaidheimh, the hill of the sword, with the fine jagged ridge of Beinn Dearg Mor to its right. Then begin to descend, gradually at first and then more steeply, into Strath na Sealga, where the track turns sharply right to run along above the river bank. It passes through alder wood and fords several burns and eventually comes to the old cottages of Achneigie, where the track ends. Behind the buildings lies a delightful waterfall.

4. Carry on the continuing footpath along the mountain-girt valley, with the Abhainn Srath na Sealga to your left. Follow the path as it steadily bears right and uphill to Shenavall bothy. Go on uphill directly behind the building and then climb steeply by the burn; it is quite scrambly in places but there is usually a choice of paths and it is nowhere difficult. As you go you might spot grey wagtails, flitting about the rocks in the burn or beside it. Low crags beyond the hurrying water obscure the view in that direction – the best view is behind you.

5. As you emerge on to the moor, where you might disturb grouse rising with a startling whirr, the path becomes boggy and spreads. Take care to keep with the line of the path, especially where you have crossed great sandstone slabs and it may not be clear where you should come off on to the peat again. A line of low crags runs parallel with the path, on the right, and these will help you locate the elusive path, which becomes clear and rocky where you cross a burn. From now on there is no further difficulty as the way carries on to the cairn mentioned earlier. Join your outward track and follow it back downhill to Corrie Hallie.

Practicals

Type of walk: *This is an exciting, challenging and strenuous walk. Carry good waterproofs and wear strong boots. The bothy provides shelter if the weather deteriorates, in which case you should return by your outward route. The return from Shenavall is quite eroded and boggy in places and sometimes indistinct. It should not be attempted in the mist.*

Distance: 11 miles/17.5km
Time: 5–6 hours
Map: OS Explorer 436/OS Landranger 19

34

Sgurr Mhor and Beinn Liath Mhor Fannaich

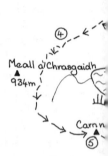

Park in a small car park, GR253755, at the west end of Loch Droma, off the A835 Garve to Ullapool road (the Dirrie More).

The **Fannaichs**, a range of mountains, lie to the south of the Dirrie More, the road over the bleak moorland from Garve to Ullapool. There are nine Munros in total, giving high level walking over short turf and moss, and well supplied with stalkers' paths. To the north they are hollowed out into fine corries, with gentler slopes to the south, down to Loch Fannach – unfortunately this side is fairly inaccessible. Seven of the Munros form a fairly continuous ridge, with the other two separated by a drop to 550m. Some very fit walkers do them all in one long day.

Beinn Liath Mhor Fannaich
and Sgurr Mor, Loch a' Mhadaidh

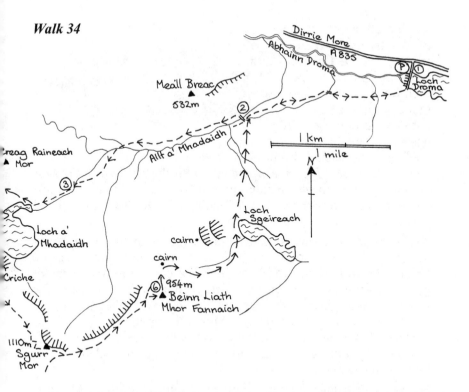

1. Cross the dam and walk the track beside the water pipe, past a small building where the huge pipe stops. Go on along the continuing track and follow it as it crosses a small burn and up into the valley of the Allt a'Mhadaidh.

2. At a fork in the track, where you can see a small dam ahead, take the right fork, go down to cross a bridge over the burn and continue up the far side. Here look for buzzards, and also peregrines performing acrobatics around the broken cliffs on Meall Breac, to your right. Walk on until you reach an old turning circle, where the track stops. Carry on along the on-going path as it descends to cross the Allt a'Mhadaidh once more and continue up the other side. Follow the distinct path through heather, where it is boggy, and comes to the side of the burn again. Cross on big rock slabs – easy when the burn is not too high, but may curtail your walk if in spate.

3. The clear path continues but pick your way carefully as it goes up and down following the river bank. Go on for 1km until you reach a flat boggy area where the burn flows out of Loch a'Mhadaidh. The stretch of water immediately in front is not the loch but the first of

an interconnected series of pools downstream from the loch. Do not try to cross over to the loch but turn right and make your way across pathless boggy ground past the pools, heading for the low ridge ahead. Look back from here to

Mossy Cyphel

admire the view of Loch a'Mhadaidh with the cliffs of Sgurr Mor behind. At the top of the ridge pick up a clear path and turn left along it. The views over to An Teallach, with Destitution Road snaking over the moor, are superb.

4. As the ground steepens the path begins to zigzag up the lower slopes of Meall a'Chrasgaidh,.to the col between the latter and Carn na Criche. From here head left to climb the easy, grassy and rocky ground to the top of Carn na Criche. Look here, in season, for moss campion, thrift and greeny-yellow mossy cyphel among the rocks, and enjoy the view of Sgurr Mor enticing you onwards. From here you have another good view. To the left look down on Loch a'Mhadaidh and, to the right, to see the spectacular cliffs below Sgurr nan Clach Geala

5. Follow the path down from the summit to the col before Sgurr Mor, and then continue up to its peak. This is the highest point in the Fannaichs – the path to its top is probably the steepest climb of the entire walk, but it is in no way difficult and is quite short. It is crowned with a substantial cairn, perched on the edge of the cliffs behind Loch a'Mhadaidh. After a suitable rest, carry on down the far side, taking the left path at a fork and so keeping fairly close to the cliff edge. Head for the long ridge linking Sgurr Mhor with Beinn Liath Mhor Fannaich, the rounded quartzite-covered peak which sticks out northwards from the rest of the range. As you descend the ground becomes less steep and here it is worth looking for a stalker's path which comes round onto this ridge from the main Fannaich ridge. Follow this path round a small rise and carry on in the same direction after the path disappears, keeping to the crest of the ridge as best you can. Cross a col before the ground begins to rise again to Beinn Liath Mhor Fannaich where you pick up the stalkers' path again. It goes left of the summit but by following it to the highest point you can avoid a lot of shattered quartzite. Eventually you have to leave the path and pick your best way over the boulders for a short distance to reach the top.

6. Two spurs protrude from the summit. Take the one going north which is somewhat lower than the other, which points north-east. Make your way down over the rough boulder-strewn ground using grassy strips where possible, until you reach the level top of the spur. Walk along it towards an obvious cairn, and just before it, leave right down a grassy and rocky slope into a grassy corrie. Come down the corrie with the burn to your left so as to keep to the easiest slopes and head for Loch Sgeireach. Cross the burn before you reach the loch and go round its north west end, then cut across the level ground and descend the hillside, heading directly, across a trackless heathery area, for the small dam and bridge on Allt a'Mhadaidh. This is where you crossed the burn on your outward route. Turn right and retrace your steps to the car park.

Practicals

Type of walk: *This is a long strenuous climb but is nowhere difficult. Much of it is on good tracks and stalkers' paths. There is a little tedious scrambling over quartzite boulder fields. It is, of course, up two Munros and all the usual cautions apply.*

Distance: 10½ miles/16.7km

Time: 6–7 hours

Maps: OS Explorer 436/OS Landranger 20

NB. Deer stalking of stags takes place here from mid-September to October 20. There is a notice about it at the road end of the Loch Droma dam.

35

Lael Forest

Park in the Lael forest car park, on the east side of the A835, opposite Auchindrean bridge, GR 196806.

The **forest garden** extends to 7 hectares and was set aside in 1933 to accommodate interesting and ornamental trees of native and foreign origin. Both the botanist and the forester have a professional interest in the performance of introduced exotic trees from which it may be possible to select timber trees of the future for further testing.

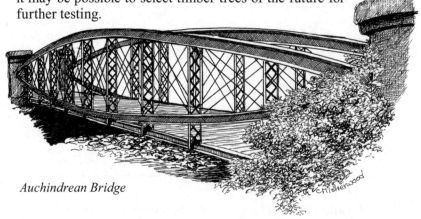

Auchindrean Bridge

1. From the corner of the car park, walk along the red and green way-marked trail. Go through a tall kissing gate and turn right onto a green waymarked path. Follow this through a plantation of mature Douglas fir, underlaid with wood sorrel and ferns, and then cross a bridge over the Allt an Earrochd. Carry on down through a kissing gate and over a bridge to the most southerly car park on the edge of the forest.

2. Cross the parking area and take the track out on the far side. The way curves round to join a forest track below a huge Sitka spruce. Turn left and go up the track through a gate in the deer fence. Beyond,

the path divides. Take the left fork and climb gently up the mossy track. Go on where it levels out and then continues as a shelf along the hillside through mature conifers, where you might spot coal tit, spotted flycatcher and siskin.

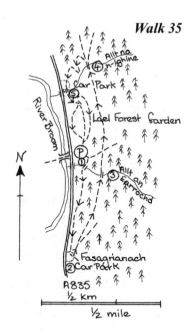

3. Cross a substantial bridge over the Allt an Earrochd, here in a deep ravine. Press on to a cross of tracks, where you continue straight ahead. Follow the red markers past scots pines to the left and where the forest is open enough to give views across Strath More to the hills beyond. On the right is an open bracken-covered hillside. Head on into denser conifers and then more open larch.

4. Cross the bridge over the Allt na h-Ighine, also in a ravine, with a waterfall almost below the bridge. Once across take a stepped path down to the left, following the red and white waymarkers. The way then continues in zig-zags through a pleasing open pinewood, with the burn on the left beyond a rail and post fence. Look over the fence for glimpses of little waterfalls. Turn left at the bottom, following the white arrows, and go through a kissing gate and down a long flight of steps to the most northerly car park.

5. Cross the bridge over the Allt na h-Ighine and go through the gate into the Lael Forest Garden. Take any of the paths to bring you back to your starting point, enjoying the splendid trees on the way.

Practicals
Type of walk: *A delightful, easy walk, which is well waymarked. It is full of interest and has some fine views.*

Distance:	2½ miles/4km
Time:	1–1½ hours
Maps:	OS Explorer 436/OS Landranger 20

36

Ullapool and Loch Achall

Park in the free car park at the end of Latheron Lane, Ullapool, next to the supermarket, GR 125942.

In 1788 the British Fisheries Society bought **Ullapool** farm from Lord MacLeod to establish herring fishing stations on Loch Broom, and a town for the workers. The town was built on a grid pattern of wide streets, the buildings planned by David Aitken, with advice from Thomas Telford. The people who settled here were mostly fishermen but merchants, tradesmen and labourers came too. Each was given a plot of land for a house and a vegetable garden. They also received a share of the common grazing.

Ullapool village clock stands in Quay Street and is reputed to be the most photographed clock in the Highlands. It originally stood in the middle of the road between the Caledonian Hotel and the corner of Quay Street and Argyle Street. It was erected in memory of the sons and a grandson of Sir John Fowler of Braemore, who were killed in action.

Ullapool harbour

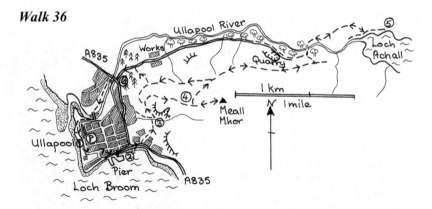

1. Leave the car park by the alley at the end, turn left and then take the second left into West Argyle Street. Here you will pass the Ceilidh Place, and then the Ullapool Museum in the old Thomas Telford church. At the junction with Quay Street admire the clock and then turn right down to the pier and enjoy the colourful fishing boats.

2. Walk along Shore Street enjoying the views of the busy harbour until you are opposite the filling station. Cross the main road (A836) here and go up the metalled road to the right of the Royal Hotel. At the end of the road is a driveway to a house, marked 'Private', and a path leading off across open ground just to the left of its fence. Go on along the path as it climbs quite steeply through birch, rowan and sycamore trees, to a kissing gate giving access to more open hillside, with scattered rowan and gorse. The path winds round the hillside and crosses a bridge over the burn issuing from a rocky (quartzite) ravine. Continue along the path to its junction with another path coming uphill, and turn right.

3. Follow this path round a hairpin bend and along the hillside, climbing gently, to a seat from which there is a splendid view of Ullapool – its grid plan can clearly be seen. Take the path to the right at the junction just before the seat and climb on up the hill. At the next junction turn left, and then very soon, right, to climb the hill ahead, Meall Mhor, 300m. It is a delightful rocky knoll, provided with yet another seat and a magnificent view of Loch Broom and Loch Achall.

Yellow Mountain Saxifrage

127

4. Retrace your footsteps to the path you left in order to climb the hill, and turn right. Join a path coming in on your left – this is your return route. Carry on gently downhill, on what is now an old hill track. Go through a kissing gate in a deer fence where, in spring and summer, yellow mountain saxifrage and heath spotted orchids thrive. Go on along the hillside. Below, left, is a working quarry; it produces lime used mainly in agriculture and which is exported all over

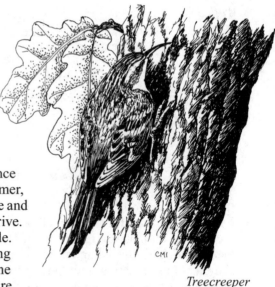

Treecreeper

Scotland. The influence of the Durness limestone on the vegetation can be seen clearly on the opposite hillside where there is a large green fertile area. Carry on along the track to another kissing gate in the deer fence and then down to a reinforced track. Turn left and very shortly right onto the metalled road to Rhiddoroch. Cross the bridge over the Ullapool River and follow the road round to reach the shores of Loch Achall. (The bridge shown on the OS map nearer to the loch no longer exists.)

5. When you are ready to return, retrace your steps along the road to the path you came down on. Go back along it beyond the second kissing gate to the Y-junction of paths noted on the outward walk. Take the right branch. At first it appears narrow, but soon becomes a wider, clearer old hill path, contouring above the valley of the Ullapool River. Shortly after passing above the stone-crushing works (associated with the quarry) the path bends sharply left and a smaller, newly made path goes off right. Take this and follow it steeply downhill across a hillside which has been planted with native trees – Scots pine, oak and alder. Turn left where it meets the Rhiddoroch estate road coming down through the quarry workings, cross the cattle grid and walk downhill to the main road.

6. Cross the A-road and turn right immediately to cross a footbridge over the Ullapool River, just below the main road bridge, where the river flows though a little gorge. Continue to the housing estate road on the far side, turn left, then immediately left again across a neat patch of mown grass with low wooden barriers at intervals across it. Descend the concrete steps and follow the delightful path which runs beside the river where the bank supports rowan and alder. At the end emerge past more wooden barricades and turn left on a tarmacked path alongside the football field. Cross the Ullapool River again on another wooden bridge, turn right and follow the other bank until you reach the 'Ullagolf' course. Walk along the track round the edge of the golf course until it goes up to join the road (West Terrace) at the start of the campsite. A little further down this road is the alleyway which takes you back to the car park.

Heath Spotted orchis

Practicals

Type of walk: *A pleasing hill walk with fine views and an interesting stroll through Ullapool.*

Distance: 5–6 miles/9–10km
Time: 2–3 hours
Map: OS Explorer 436/OS Landrangers 19 and 20

37

Dun Canna

Park in a small car park that lies at the end of a rough track, GR 135015. To reach this take the signposted minor road to Blughasary, 7 miles north of Ullapool. Drive for 1 mile down the road, where grass grows along its middle, and carry on when it becomes a cart track. The car park is at the end, labelled 'Dun Canna, walkers car park'.

The site of the **fort, Dun Canna**, is strategically placed on a delightful peninsula, jutting out into the sea, with curving bays on either side. In summer wheatears flit about the boulders and English stonecrop grows along the path. To the left lies Isle Martin, with the ruins of an extensive fish curing station and the remains of the chapel of St Martin.

River Runie, Blughasary

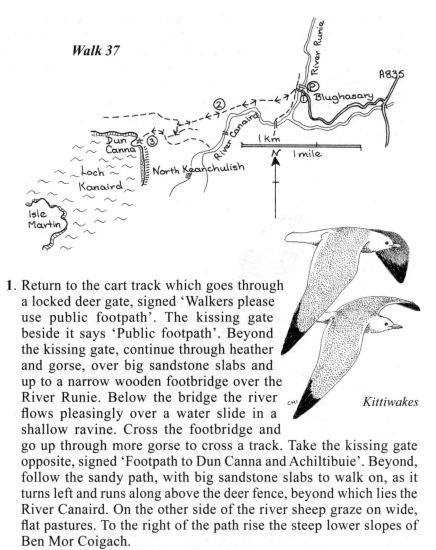

Kittiwakes

1. Return to the cart track which goes through a locked deer gate, signed 'Walkers please use public footpath'. The kissing gate beside it says 'Public footpath'. Beyond the kissing gate, continue through heather and gorse, over big sandstone slabs and up to a narrow wooden footbridge over the River Runie. Below the bridge the river flows pleasingly over a water slide in a shallow ravine. Cross the footbridge and go up through more gorse to cross a track. Take the kissing gate opposite, signed 'Footpath to Dun Canna and Achiltibuie'. Beyond, follow the sandy path, with big sandstone slabs to walk on, as it turns left and runs along above the deer fence, beyond which lies the River Canaird. On the other side of the river sheep graze on wide, flat pastures. To the right of the path rise the steep lower slopes of Ben Mor Coigach.

2. Continue along the path where well placed railway sleepers enable the walker to cross fairly dry-shod. Go on to cross a boggy area, with ahead splendid views of Beinn Ghoblach and also of An Teallach further left. Carry on to a cairn on a slab marking a path which climbs steeply up the hillside, signposted 'To Achiltibuie, dangerous path'. Ignore this path and take the left branch, over more sleepers to continue to a kissing gate in the deer fence. Beyond, walk on over more sleepers to a track where you turn right. Stride on to a T-junction. Here turn right, go through a gate and follow the grassy track as it curves round below cliffs to come to a mass of sandstone boulders, originally part of a wall, the site of Dun Canna. Ahead in the bay you can see Isle Martin. Here you might see kittiwakes returning to their nests after catching surface-swimming fish.

3. To return, retrace your steps. Do not be tempted to use the grassy level tracks on the river side of the deer fence because the gates at the end are padlocked and topped with barbed wire.

Buzzard

Practicals

Type of walk: *A pleasing walk through delightful countryside – especially after a dry spell. Dramatic views.*

Distance: 4 miles/6.5km
Time: 2 hours
Maps: OS Explorer 439/OS Landranger 15

38

Knockan Cliff Geological Trail

Park in the visitor centre, GR 188092. To reach this take the A835 north from Ullapool in the direction of Ledmore Junction.

Knockan Cliff is famous in geological circles for its splendid exposure of the Moine Thrust. This is a fault which was formed where two land masses collided and one was pushed over the top of the other. The lower rocks here are, first, Cambrian quartzite and then, Durness limestone on top of it. They lie on top of the Torridon sandstone and below that is the Lewisian gneiss, both of which are Pre-Cambrian. Above the Durness limestone is a narrow region of ground-up rock (mylonite, formed by the movement of one rock mass over another) and then the Moine schists, which are also Pre-Cambrian and much older that the limestone below them. You can put your hands, one on each side of the fault, and touch rocks millions of years different in age, with the younger ones lowest. The fault has a dip of about 10 degres only. The Moine rocks probably came from thousands of kilometres away – beyond present-day Scandinavia – and cannot be related to the Torridonian and Lewisian rocks even though they are all of Pre-Cambrian age.

View from Knockan

Durness limestone was formed in a clear sea which was inhabited by various animals whose remains occur sparsely as fossils. At Knockan it forms the narrow band of white outcrops at the foot of the summit cliff. It produces lime-rich soil, which is generally very fertile, supporting lush plant life and vivid green grass. The nearby brown peaty areas, supporting poor moorland grass and heather, occur where there is no limestone.

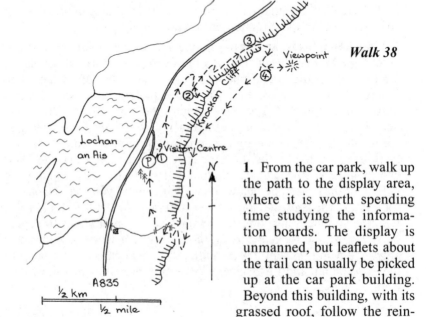

Walk 38

1. From the car park, walk up the path to the display area, where it is worth spending time studying the information boards. The display is unmanned, but leaflets about the trail can usually be picked up at the car park building. Beyond this building, with its grassed roof, follow the reinforced path to the first junction, where you turn left and descend slightly. Take the first side path, on the left, which leads you to a flat area where you can inspect samples of pipe rock, brought up here from lower down the hillside. This pipe rock is Cambrian quartzite (a very pure sandstone) full of fossilised worm tubes. Return to the main path which begins to climb. Admire the fine spherical sculpture, on your right, as you go down to an attractive wooden bridge over a tiny burn. Look at the rock layers exposed here, then climb up to another exposure higher up. Where the path divides, do not take the return path to the car park, but carry on up the main trail.

2. Climb up steps to a detour on the right leading to another exposure. Here you can see the Moine schists overlying the Durness limestone.

The difference in the rock types is very obvious, and it is amazing to think that it is where the older schist has been forced over the younger rocks by immense earth movements. Go back down to the main path and turn right along it. It contours the hillside for a while, below the cliffs. Look at the vegetation as you walk – you are on limestone here and will, in summer, see lots of lime-loving plants – thyme in abundance, yellow mountain saxifrage, fairy flax, St John's wort and a few clumps of the beautiful mountain avens.

3. Climb very steeply up the crag on the recently repaired, solid stone steps. The path turns right at the top and a branch to the left goes to a splendid viewpoint. Look for the Ben More Assynt massif to the north, with all the mountains capped in grey quartzite Look also for Suilven, Cul Mor and Cul Beag to the west, rearing up out of the low-lying land of the Inverpolly and Drumrunie forests. The vegetation here on the crag is much more acid-loving – heather, wavy hair grass, viviparous fescue, mat grass and tormentil.

4. Return to the stone and gravel path, solid and well made, which follows the cliff edge. There is another sculpture on a high point on your left and directly below is the car park. Through the gap between Cul Mor and Cul Beag you can see the spectacular shape of Stac Pollaidh (see Walk 39) and the low ground all around is studded with lochans. At a break in the cliffs the path descends in well graded zigzags. It crosses the limestone briefly and then goes through a few trees to the car park.

Mountain Avens

Practicals

Type of walk: *A geological delight*

Distance:	1–1½ miles/1.8–2.5km
Time:	1 hour
Maps:	OS Explorer 439/OS Landranger 15

39

Stac Pollaidh

Park in the car park, GR 107095, on the south side of the minor road from Drumrunie to Achiltibuie where it passes below Stac Pollaidh.

The distinctive shape of **Stac Pollaidh** makes it instantly recognisable. It has two craggy summits linked by a jagged ridge. Because of the excessive erosion caused by the mountain's popularity together with the fact that it is very steep and made of relatively soft sandstone, the path has been remade. It is now pitched and follows the line of the old path to the plateau. It then heads off east. You are asked not to attempt to climb straight up the front.

Stac Pollaidh lies within the **Inverpolly National Nature Reserve**. It is one of the largest reserves in Britain, ranging from offshore islands and coasts, to upland corries and glens. It embraces some of

Cul Mor from Stac Pollaidh

the most rugged, spectacular scenery in Scotland. The combination of loch, mountain, woodland and moorland supports a great variety of plant and animal life. The reserve is managed by the Scottish Natural Heritage in cooperation with the the three estates it covers.

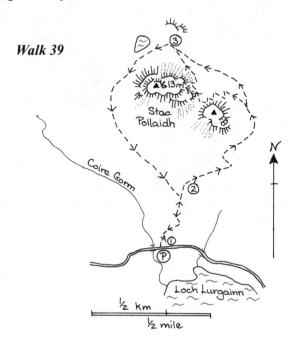

Walk 39

1. Cross the road and go through the gate opposite the car park. Follow the pitched path through several birch trees and then follow the way as it climbs steadily to a small plateau. Ignore the path going off left (your return route) and continue on to pass through the gate in the erosion control fencing. From here there is a good view of the Western Isles.

2. Head on up, following the path as it bears slightly right and then left up a shallow valley. Here you might spot the white rumps of wheatears as they flit away from the rocks on your approach. The path then goes quite steeply, but well stepped, round the east end of the hill. At a Y-junction of paths you have a choice. The left branch climbs steadily, making a large zig-zag to come to the ridge between the two huge, rocky outlandish turrets, where a breathtaking view awaits. The right branch traverses below the summit and also below the large fenced area where serious past erosion is beginning to recover. The view, on

this side of the mountain, from both paths, is of a glorious patchwork of lochs, part of the Inverpolly National Nature Reserve It is as if you are viewing a relief map. Beyond lie the tops of Quinag, Canisp, Suilven and Cul Mor. From the ridge continue on above the erosion control fence and then gently descend. If on lower path, go on with the fencing to your left.

Wheatear

3. At the west end of Stac Pollaidh both paths join. Carry on winding round the side of the mountain and follow the path, equally well restored, as it goes drops quite steeply. It then traverses the front (south side) before gently descending to join the main path just below the deer gate passed through early on during the walk. Follow your outward path down the slopes and through the birches to the road and the car park.

Practicals

Type of walk: *A wonderfully exhilarating climb with the choice of a circuit around the bizarre shaped hill.or a climb to the ridge and then on along the circuit. The whole route is well reinforced and graded.*

Distance: 1½ miles/2.5km
Time: 2 hours
Maps: OS Explorer 439/OS Landranger 15

40

Reiff

Park at Reiff, GR 965145, on the left side of a track which continues ahead at the point where the road swings sharp left to come to an abrupt end by the bridge over the outflow from the Loch of Reiff. There is room for several cars but take care not to impede access to the cottages beyond. There is also parking for four more on the right of the road immediately before the bridge – much frequented by anglers and rock climbers; best get there early. To reach Reiff, take the A835, north of Ullapool. Turn west at Drumrunie, signposted Achiltibuie. Ignore the right turn to Lochinver and continue to a T-junction beside Loch Raa. Turn right for Achnahaird and Altandhu. Go over a hill and down the far side to Altandhu where you turn right at another T-junction. Continue to the road at Reiff.

The **Torridonian sandstone cliffs** at Reiff are very popular with rock climbers, being sound clean rocks, and the routes are quite short. It is a good place for everyone – beginners and experts alike. You will probably see several groups on the sea cliffs around the small hill to the west of the Loch of Reiff.

Camas Eilean Ghlais, Reiff

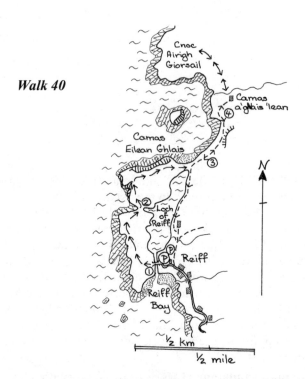

Walk 40

1. Follow the road to its end and cross the outflow from the loch on the wide bridge. Go through the gate at the far side and make your way slightly right over the short turf towards the sea. In summer the grass is full of flowers – devil's-bit scabious, tormentil, thyme, and heather and it is a delight to walk. Look out to sea for fulmars and gannets, and sometimes for kittiwakes if the weather is windy. Great skuas and occasionally Arctic skuas use Loch of Reiff as a flightpath and can be seen here regularly in summer – large, dark and fast causing terror among the gulls (see Walk 29). Walk on along the high ground behind the sandstone blocks of the shore, then descend to a wet inlet between the sea and the loch which you can cross easily on stones.

2. Take the small path on the far side which leads up round the head of a fine chasm to the highest point (20m). Walk around the top of the cliffs and admire the view of the next bay, Camas Eilean Ghlais. It has a fine rock stack of an island in the middle, and you are likely to see shags and black guillemots around it. In autumn the bay often holds two or

three long-tailed duck, and you might also see an otter. Follow the path downhill into the bay, stepping over the fence, where everyone else has done, and crossing over the top (north end) of the Loch of Reiff.

3. Follow the continuing path along a shelf above the beach and then go down to a storm beach of cobbles, before finally winding round a corner and up to the isolated cottage of Camas a'ghlais'lean. At this point if you want to extend the walk you could go onto the next headland and up to the high ground of Cnoc Airigh Giorsail, or all the way to Rubha Coigeach, but the way does become much rougher.

4. To continue this walk, retrace your steps to the low point at the end of Loch of Reiff. Here take a narrow somewhat rough path going along the east shore of the loch. Here you might see mergansers and sandpipers, the latter frequenting the shore in spring and summer. The path keeps to the lochside below a cottage and then comes up the bank to join the track where you may have parked.

Drake long-tailed ducks in autumn

Practicals

Type of walk: *A very satisfactory short walk.*

Distance: 2 miles/3.4km
Time: 2 hours
Maps: OS Explorer 439/OS Landranger 15

Walking Scotland Series
from Clan Books

MARY WELSH has already compiled walkers' guides to each of the areas listed: material for guides covering the remaining parts of Scotland is being gathered for publication in future volumes.

Titles published so far:

1. WALKING THE ISLE OF ARRAN
2. WALKING THE ISLE OF SKYE
3. WALKING WESTER ROSS
4. WALKING PERTHSHIRE
5. WALKING THE WESTERN ISLES
6. WALKING ORKNEY
7. WALKING SHETLAND
8. WALKING THE ISLES OF ISLAY, JURA AND COLONSAY
9. WALKING GLENFINNAN: THE ROAD TO THE ISLES
10. WALKING THE ISLES OF MULL, IONA, COLL AND TIREE
11. WALKING DUMFRIES AND GALLOWAY
12. WALKING ARGYLL AND BUTE
13. WALKING DEESIDE, DONSIDE AND ANGUS
14. WALKING THE TROSSACHS, LOCH LOMONDSIDE AND THE CAMPSIE FELLS
15. WALKING GLENCOE, LOCHABER AND THE GREAT GLEN
16. WALKING STRATHSPEY, MORAY, BANFF AND BUCHAN
17. WALKING AROUND LOCH NESS, THE BLACK ISLE AND EASTER ROSS
18. WALKING CAITHNESS AND SUTHERLAND
19. WALKING THE SCOTTISH BORDERS AND EAST LOTHIAN

Books in this series can be ordered through booksellers anywhere.
In the event of difficulty write to
Clan Books, The Cross, DOUNE, FK16 6BE, Scotland.

For more details, visit the Clan Books website at
www.walkingscotlandseries.co.uk